POETRY, LANGUAGE, THOUGHT

MARTIN HEIDEGGER
WORKS

General Editor J. Glenn Gray
Colorado College

———

Also by Martin Heidegger

BEING AND TIME

DISCOURSE ON THINKING
(Gelassenheit)

WHAT IS CALLED THINKING?

IDENTITY AND DIFFERENCE

HEGEL'S CONCEPT OF EXPERIENCE

ON THE WAY TO LANGUAGE

POETRY, LANGUAGE, THOUGHT

MARTIN HEIDEGGER

Translations and Introduction by
Albert Hofstadter

1817

HARPER & ROW, PUBLISHERS

New York, Evanston, San Francisco, London

LIBRARY OF CONGRESS CATALOG CARD NUMBER: 79-161639

CONTENTS

PREFACE

I have benefited enormously—the word is not strong enough —from the generosity of J. Glenn Gray in recurrently reviewing the translations down to their last details. Professor Gray's work with Heidegger on them, renewed over and over again, gives me the assurance that they may be submitted to the reading public with the feeling that at least some of Heidegger's own thinking comes through.

Hannah Arendt has been particularly liberal with suggestions for improvement; the present text contains many changes due to her.

Here and there are some verses—of Heidegger himself and also of C. F. Meyer, Rilke, Trakl, and Hölderlin. Because of the closeness with which Heidegger treats other poets, they needed original translation, and so for good or ill and *faute de mieux* they are all from my own hand.

In addition to the enduring and tireless encouragement of my son Marc and my wife Manya, I have special reason to refer here with love and gratitude to Evelyn Huber, whose courage and loyalty those know best who have come within her gentle sphere.

Santa Cruz, California   ALBERT HOFSTADTER

INTRODUCTION

Assembled in this book are seven writings that seem to be directly or indirectly concerned with art. But appearances can be deceiving.

These pieces should not be thought of under the heading of "aesthetics," nor even under that of "philosophy of art."

Heidegger's thinking about art is not concerned with the work of art as the object of *aisthesis,* that is, of the sensuous apprehension, in the wide sense, which goes by the name of aesthetic experience. His estimate of the significance of such experience, and a fortiori of aesthetics, can be judged from the Epilogue to "The Origin of the Work of Art." And his thinking, not only about art but about all else as well, is not philosophy in the sense of metaphysics, or of a universal theory about the nature and characteristics of things that exist, whether art works or anything else. His estimate of philosophy may be gauged from the remark in "The Thinker as Poet" (p. 8) that, of the three dangers threatening thinking, the bad and thus muddled one is philosophizing.

Heidegger's thinking about art, as about all else, is—a thinking that memorializes and responds, *ein andenkendes Denken.* Like poetry and song, it grows out of being and reaches into its truth ("The Thinker as Poet," p. 13). The being that is its origin is the being to which authentic human being belongs. Some understanding of its nature will be gleaned from Heidegger's accounts, in several of the essays, of the being of world, of thing, of art work, of man, of language.

One should first of all, perhaps, note his advice to the young student, Mr. Buchner, who had asked whence thinking about Being receives its directive ("The Thing," pp. 183f). To think being, Heidegger says, means to respond to the appeal of its presence, in a response that stems from and releases itself toward the appeal. But this means to exist as a human being in an authentic relationship as mortal to other mortals, to earth and sky, to the divinities present or absent, to things and plants and animals; it means, to let each of these be—to let it presence in openness, in the full appropriateness of its nature—and to hold oneself open to its being, recognizing it and responding to it appropriately in one's own being, the way in which one oneself goes on, lives; and then, perhaps, in this ongoing life one may hear the call of the language that speaks of the being of all these beings and respond to it in a mortal language that speaks of what it hears.

To understand how man may think in this way, recalling to mind the being that has, according to Heidegger, long been concealed in oblivion, one must understand the nature of the language by which thinking is able to say what it thinks. Hence the inclusion of "Language," the first essay in *Unterwegs zur Sprache*. The speech of genuine thinking is by nature *poetic*. It need not take the shape of verse; as Heidegger says, the opposite of the poem is not prose; pure prose is as poetic as any poetry. The voice of thought must be poetic because poetry is the saying of truth, the saying of the unconcealedness of beings ("The Origin of the Work of Art," p. 74). It bids all that is—world and things, earth and sky, divinities and mortals—to come, gathering into the simple onefold of their intimate belonging together. ("Language," pp. 206f). It is the topology of being, telling being the whereabouts of its actual presence ("The Thinker as Poet," p. 12).

Is there in the end any fundamental difference between the thinking poet and the poetic thinker? The poet need not think; the thinker need not create poetry; but to be a poet of first rank there is a thinking that the poet must accomplish, and it is the same kind of thinking, in essence, that the thinker of first rank must accomplish, a thinking which has all the purity and thickness and solidity of poetry, and whose saying *is* poetry. In these essays, as they advance in date of composition, one may discern at the same time an increase in the poetic quality of their language. It is not an accident; it goes along with the growth of the author's vision of truth and being, and of man's life in the context of truth and being. In order to say what he must say, reporting what he sees, relaying what he hears, the author has to speak of the gods, mortals, the earth, shoes, the temple, the sky, the bridge, the jug, the fourfold, the poem, pain, the threshold, the difference, and stillness as he does. In truth, this is not philosophy; it is not abstract theorizing about the problems of knowledge, value, or reality; it is the most concrete thinking and speaking about Being, the differing being of different beings and the onefoldness of their identity in and with all their differences; and it is one with the being of the thinker and speaker, himself. In this thinking, which is the thinking that responds and recalls—*das andenkende Denken*—the thinker has stepped back from thinking that merely represents, merely explains, and has taken up his stance in "a co-responding which, appealed to in the world's being by the world's being, answers within itself to that appeal" (*"The Thing,"* pp. 181f).

Out of the experience of such thinking comes the first piece. I have entitled it in English "The Thinker as Poet" because in it the thinker does what a poet does—*dichtet*. We have no word for it in English. I had tried "poetize" for *dichten,* but it has the wrong connotation and excites annoyance in those who feel for the language, suggesting affectation. *Dichten*—to write or compose poetry or other literature; to invent something fictional, make it up, imagine it. So it gets translated rather as poetry, or the writing of poetry, and often, where the word "poetry" appears, it is well to remember its sense as a verb, as naming the act of composing and writing—as, for example, in "The Thinker as Poet" (p. 13), where poetry is the activity that corresponds in a neighborly way to singing and thinking.

Heidegger's original title for this piece was *Aus der Erfahrung des Denkens*—"From the Experience of Thinking"—and one should read it as such, as the uttering of realizations that have come out of a long life of discovery of a way of thinking that belongs to life in its fullness as genuinely human. Every sentence in this thinking poem is pregnant with meaning. He who has read the entire book and then returns to it will find that what first seemed new, strange, difficult, now rings out with the clarity of a purely-wrought bell, letting one begin to hear the voice of thought, stilled in its being by having become unable to say what must remain unspoken; it is a speaking that, like all genuine poetry, says more than it speaks, means more than it utters. Perhaps then the reader will, some fine moment, understand what it means to say: *Segen sinnt*—"Blessing muses."

This poem fittingly begins a series of essays in which a main theme is that poetry opens the dwelling life of man. In "The Origin of the Work of Art" (1935–36) Heidegger had already pointed to the function of poetry as the founding of truth: bestowing, grounding, beginning. He conceived of poetry as projective utterance—"the saying of world and earth, the saying of the arena of their conflict and thus of the place of all nearness and remoteness of the gods . . . the saying of the unconcealedness of what is" (p. 74). This understanding of poetry remains throughout and is more and more developed as his writing progresses.

From early to late, too, we find the comprehension of the fundamental identity of art and language with poetry. All art, we learn from "The Origin of the Work of Art," is essentially poetry, because it is the letting happen of the advent of the truth of what is ("Origin," p. 72). And poetry, as linguistic, has a privileged position in the domain of the arts, because language, understood rightly, is the original way in which beings are brought into the open clearing of truth, in which world and earth, mortals and gods are bidden to come to their appointed places of meeting ("Origin," pp. 74f).

Authentic language, which has not lost its magical potency by being used up and abused, is poetry; there is no significant difference between them. That is why, when Heidegger attempts to state in the essay "Language" what language is and does, namely, what it does when it speaks, he chooses something "spoken purely," rather than any random spoken matter. What is spoken purely is—a poem, and indeed, to help us best a poem that shows in its very speaking what language does when it speaks: Georg Trakl's "A Winter Evening."

Through the reading of this poem we become aware of how language, in speaking, bids to come the entire fourfold world of earth and sky, mortals and divinities, by bidding the things to come—window, snow, house, table—that stay the world, and bidding the world to come that grants things their being; it bids to come the intimacy of world and things—their difference, which appropriates them to one another. What unites opposites is the rift, the *Riss* (cf. "Origin") that has become the dif-ference, the pain of the threshold that joins. ("Language," p. 204).

Whether Heidegger speaks of truth establishing itself in the beings that it opens up (*"Origin,"* p. 63) or of world and things being joined through the pain of the rift of their dif-ference, he is thinking always of the opening up of the possibility of authentic human existence—of a life in which man does not merely go on blindly, writhing in the grip of a basically false meaning of being, as in our twentieth-century life of *Gestell,* framing, but rather a life in which man truly *dwells.*

Dwelling is one of the basic thoughts in these writings. In "Building Dwelling Thinking"—note the absence of commas, intended to enforce the identity of the three—Heidegger develops the essential continuity of being, building, dwelling, and thinking. Language makes the connection for us: *bauen,* to build, connects with *buan* to dwell, and with *bin, bist,* the words for be. Language tells us: to be a human being is to be on the earth as a mortal, to dwell, doing the "building" that belongs to dwelling: cultivating growing things, constructing things that are built, and doing all this in the context of mortals who, living on earth and cherishing it, look to the sky and to the gods to find the measure of their dwelling. If man's being is dwelling, and if man must look to the way the world fits together to find the measure by which he can determine his dwelling life, then man must dwell poetically.

So in what Heidegger cites as a late poem of Hölderlin's, the one beginning "In lovely blueness blooms the steeple with metal roof," there occurs the phrase ". . . poetically man dwells . . ." which becomes the subject of the final essay in this volume. For how the world fits together, the appropriating of mortals to divinities, earth to sky, things to places and functions—how all is rightly measured out—can be determined only by the upward glance that spans the between of earth and sky, the dimension. It is poetry that takes the measure of the dimension, that is the standard by which all other measures—of this or that or something else—are themselves measured. The poet it is who, looking to the sky, sees in its manifestness the self-concealment of the unknown god, bidding the unknown to come to man to help him dwell. At the basis of man's ability to build in the sense of cultivating and constructing there must be, as primal source, his poetic ability, the ability to take the measure of the world.

Even what is apparently so simple as a simple thing—a jug, for instance, or a bridge, or a pair of peasant shoes—has to be seen in the light of the disclosure of the appropriation of beings to Being, the Open, the clearing of truth, if man's relationship to it is to be authentically human.

The remarkable essay on "The Thing" (and "thing" is another of the basic concepts in Heidegger's thought) makes indelibly clear and vivid what a thing can be—a jug, as he deals with it here, or, as he notes, a bench, a brook, a bull, a book. He takes hold of the Being of things in the concretest way, a way he learned originally from the phenomenology of Husserl, according to which one's vision is addressed to things as they show themselves in the fullness of their appearance. What was a puzzle in "The Origin of the Work of Art" becomes transparently evident in these later essays.

There is a world of difference between man's present life as technological being under the aegis of *Gestell,* frame, framing —in which everything, including man himself, becomes material for a process of self-assertive production, self-assertive imposition of human will on things regardless of their own essential natures—and a life in which he would genuinely dwell as a human being. This time of technology is a destitute time, the time of the world's night, in which man has even forgotten that he has forgotten the true nature of being. In such a dark and deprived time, it is the task of the poet to help us see once more the bright possibility of a true world. That is what poets are for, now. But it means that, as poets, they must free themselves completely from bondage to the time's idols; and Heidegger's examination in "What Are Poets For?" of the poetry of Rilke, as on the way but not yet there, as still involved in the toils of the metaphysical view of reality, is of special timeliness.

So poetry—together with the language and thinking that belong to it and are identical with it as essential poetry—has for Heidegger an indispensable function for human life: it is the creative source of the humanness of the dwelling life of man. Without the poetic element in our own being, and without our poets and their great poetry, we would be brutes, or what is worse and what we are most like today: vicious automata of self-will.

It is not aesthetics, then, that one will find in this book. Rather, it is fundamental thinking about the constitutive role that the poetic has in human life. Aesthetics, as we know it from the history of philosophy, is a talking about appearances, experiences, and judgments, useful no doubt, and agreeable. But Heidegger here thinks through the basic creative function that obtains its creativeness from its willingness to stop, listen, hear, remember, and respond to the call that comes from Being. He does here, and in all his writings, what thinking is called upon by nature to do: to open up and take true measure of the dimension of our existence.

Much could be written about the language of Heidegger's thinking. It has created its own style, as always happens with an original thinker. Often a sentence or two is all that is necessary to distinguish Heidegger from, say, Wittgenstein, Russell, or Whitehead. The style is the thinking itself. It comes out of the German language and partakes of that language's genius. Schelling and Hegel spoke proudly of the natural fitness of the German language for philosophy; and in Heidegger's writings, increasingly with their chronological advance, we have a vivid example of this aptitude. It is by staying with the thinking the language itself does that Heidegger is able to rethink, and thus think anew, the oldest, the perennial and perennially forgotten, thoughts.

This does not mean that he wilfully resorts to etymological or pseudo-etymological factors to play an arbitrary language game. He uses etymology as much to uncover human misadventures in thinking as to bring to light what has been obscured in history. An example is his account of the words for "thing"— *das Ding, res, causa, cosa, chose,* where from the fundamental original sense of "gathering" there is a movement toward "that which bears on or concerns men," "that which is present, as standing forth here," eventually leading to "anything that is in any way," anything present in any way whatever, even if only in mental representation as an *ens rationis* ("The Thing," p. 176). The ancient thought of gathering falls into oblivion as the later thought of abstract being and presence takes over and occupies the foreground of thinking. Yet the ancient thought—an original discovery of the poets and thinkers who spoke the Indo-European languages into being—is the one that is truest to the nature of the thing as it is knowable in and from living experience.

Read what Heidegger has to say about the thinging of things, that is, the gathering and uniting—or as the German says so directly and strongly, *das Verweilen,* the letting-while or letting-dwell—by which the world is stayed, in virtually every sense of "stay," and you will begin to re-collect in your own thinking a basic human grasp of the meaning of things, which will open up afresh a basic human relationship to them (e.g., the jug in "The Thing," the bridge in "Building Dwelling Thinking," the snow, the bed, the house in "Language"). As over against the modern concept of the thing which sees it primarily in its relation to human understanding as an object of representation and in its relation to human will as matter or product of a process of production or self-imposition—a concept, then, not of the thing in its own thingness, but of the thing in its sub-servience to human preoccupations—Heidegger finds in language the thought of the thing as thing, that is, as gathering and staying a world in its own special way. Hence he is able to use "thing" as a verb and, by this new coining and recoining of the ancient word and its meaning, to think recallingly and responsively the being of the thing as man has authentically lived with things from the beginning.

Call this primitivism, if you will; it can also be called a re-calling to origins, a reversion to the primeval, as Rilke describes what happens to everything perfect in one of the *Sonnets to Orpheus* (cf. "What Are Poets For?"—p. 97). It represents a movement away from the thin abstractions of representational thinking and the stratospheric constructions of scientific theorizing, and toward the full concreteness, the onefoldness of the manifold, of actual life-experience. This is the sort of response that Heidegger has made to the old cry of Husserl, "Back to the things themselves!"

Heidegger's thinking, *Denken,* is a re-thinking, *Andenken,* a recalling, remembering, memorializing, and responding to an original call coming from the central living presencing of the being of the world, and of men and other beings in the world. It calls for the complete opening of the human spirit—what otherwise gets fragmented into intellect, will, heart, and senses— to the ever-present possibilities of the truth of being, letting the world light up, clear up, join itself into one in manifold self-appropriations, letting us find in it a real dwelling place instead of the cold, sterile hostelry in which we presently find ourselves.

This is what causes the difficulties, and also the joys, of translating him. For to find the right English words one has to learn to think the German thoughts. The dictionary often is useless for this purpose. No ordinary dictionary can explain what Heidegger wants to say by *wesen, ereignen, verweilen, Gestell,* or fifty other such words. Take the verb *ereignen* with its associated noun *das Ereignis* as example. In his earlier writing, as in "Origin," he tends to use the dictionary senses—to happen, occur, take place, and event, occurrence, happening. But as time goes on, searching to find the right expression of the meaning of Being, he discovers in this word what is not present in other ontological words like *sein* and *wesen.* The sense of "to be present" that is carried by *wesen* especially in the form of *anwesen,* though weighty, is inadequate to reach the primeval. Although presence is already very important in early Greek thinking about being, it is mixed up with presence for representational perception and presence as result of a process of bringing forth and disclosing here. The problem is to express a being's *own* way of occurring, happening, being present, not just *for* our understanding, will, and perception, but as the being it itself is. And Heidegger eventually finds the answer in *ereignen.*

This discovery is a curious one and shows clearly how Heidegger's dealing with language, far from being a mere etymologizing, is a creative employment of its possibilities in order to express *de novo* thoughts that belong perennially to human life but that have been more and more clouded over by the artificialities of the modern imprisonment of man in a culture dominated by the will to power and the technical-technological brain.

In the "Addendum" (1956) to "The Origin of the Work of Art" (1935–36), and thus at a more advanced stage of his comprehension, Heidegger refers to *das Ereignis* as that by which the meaning of Being can alone be determined ("Origin," p. 86). *Das Ereignis* is *the event,* in the dictionary sense, the *happening* or *occurrence.* But this translation makes little sense in the context. The suggestion is that we can only find the meaning of Being in something called *das Ereignis.* What is this *Ereignis?*

We begin to gather the word's import for Heidegger from his use of it in a decisive passage of "The Thing" (*Vorträge und Aufsätze,* pp. 178–79), where he is concerned to describe the world and its presencing, its "worlding." This is decisive because, if Heidegger gets close to saying what the Being of beings is, taking them all together, in their world, it is in and through this description of the world's being as such, the true and sole dimension of which is "nearing" ("Thing," p. 181).

Heidegger there defines the world as: *das ereignende Spiegel-Spiel der Einfalt von Erde und Himmel, Göttlichen und Sterblichen,* "the *ereigende* mirror-play of the simple onefold of earth and sky, divinities and mortals" ("Thing," p. 179). The force of this participial adjective is given by the context. The four members of the fourfold—earth, sky, divinities, mortals— mirror each other, each in its own way. Each therewith reflects itself, in its own way, into its *Eigenes,* its own, within the simpleness of the four. The mirroring, lighting each of the four, *ereignet* their *eigenes* presencing into simple belonging to one another. It is clear that Heidegger here is making use of the "own" meaning of *"eigen"* to read the sense of the verb *ereignen* as *to make one's own, to appropriate*. But instead of "appropriate" in the sense of one's own appropriating of something for oneself, for which the verb *sich (etwas) aneignen* is already available, Heidegger wants to speak of an activity or process by which nothing "selfish" occurs, but rather by which the different members of the world are brought into belonging to and with one another and are helped to realize themselves and each other in realizing this belonging. Johannine Christianity speaks of God as Love, the love that binds spirits into true community and that is the source of all harmony of being. Heidegger finds in the world's worlding that nearing by which its fourfold can be gathered, nestling, conjoining, in a round dance of appropriating and self-appropriating, in which the four, fouring, can unite in their belonging together. *Ereignen* is the verb that names the appropriating by which there can be a meaningful mutual entrusting and belonging of the four to each other.

But that is only one side of the coin. The verb *ereignen* was not in historical fact constructed out of the prefix *er-* and the adjective *eigen,* own. There was an earlier verb *eräugnen,* to place before the eyes, to show, connected with the noun *Auge* for eye. Some pronunciations sound *äu* like *ei,* and so it became natural to sound the word as *ereignen* and thereupon to read its meaning accordingly. *Ereignis,* the noun, is similarly related to *Eräugnung, Ereignung.* Heidegger must have had this connection in mind. And it ties in with his most essential thinking. He had started, coming out of phenomenology, with the idea of truth as evidence, opening up, clearing, lighting, the self-showing of beings in overtness. This sense of truth dominates "The Origin of the Work of Art," and consequently much more emphasis is placed there on the lighting-clearing of the Open than there is on the appropriating of beings to beings, on light than on right. Similarly the art work, and a fortiori the poem, is more dominantly conceived as that in and through which truth as clearing-lighting occurs than as something in which, as in ". . . Poetically Man Dwells . . . ," the measure is taken of all measures, i.e., the basic grasp of rightness and fitness by which beings belong to one another. I do not say the difference of earlier and later thought here is absolutely sharp, but it is considerable and it is one noteworthy phase of the deepening and ripening of Heidegger's thought as he returned again and again to the problem of the thing, the work, truth, and the meaning of Being.

Thus *ereignen* comes to mean, in his writing, the joint process by which the four of the fourfold are able, first, to come out into the light and clearing of truth, and thus each to exist in its own truthful way, and secondly, to exist in appropriation of and to each other, belonging together in the round dance of their being; and what is more, this mutual appropriation becomes the very process by which the emergence into the light and clearing occurs, for it happens through the sublimely simple play of their mutual mirroring. The mutual lighting-up, reflecting, *eräugnen,* is at the same time the mutual belonging, appropriating, *ereignen;* and conversely, the happening, *das Ereignis,* by which alone the meaning of Being can be determined, is this play of *eräugnen* and *ereignen:* it is an *Eräugnen* which is an *Ereignen* and an *Ereignen* which is an *Eräugnen.*

It is because of this interpenetrating association of coming out into the open, the clearing, the light—or disclosure—with the conjunction and compliancy of mutual appropriation, that I have ventured to translate "*das Ereignis,*" in the Addendum to "Origin," not just as "the *event,*" "the *happening,*" or "the *occurrence,*" but rather as "the *disclosure of appropriation.*" This translation has survived the critical scrutiny of Heidegger himself, as well as J. Glenn Gray and Hannah Arendt, and therefore I repose a certain trust in its fitness.

And a final point on *Ereignis.* In the earlier period, when the great emphasis was on truth as evidence, on placing before the eyes, *eräugnen,* the meaning of truth was defined in terms of *das Licht,* light, *lichten,* to clear, thin out, grow brighter, and *die Lichtung,* clearing, glade, opening. But as the thinking matured, although the effect of clearing, opening, brightening, and lighting remained, there was added to it a sense associated with the adjective *leicht,* that is, light in the sense of opposed to heavy, and especially in the sense of easy, effortless, nimble. Heidegger underlines this dimension of *Lichtung* when he identifies the gathered being of the world's mirror-play as the "ringing," *das Gering*—an impossible word to translate. He indicates here how the world's ring-around dance of being is, in the old German sense, *ring, gering,* nestling, malleable, pliant, compliant, *leicht,* that is, light, easy, nimble ("The Thing," p. 180; *Vorträge und Aufsätze,* p. 179).

Thus the older coming out into the clearing of truth now becomes the conjoining in the mirror-play of mutual appropriation which *lightens* all the four into their own; and therefore I have translated *"lichtend,"* which in "Origin" would have been "clearing," now as "lightening," intending it to bear at once and in inseparable union the senses of: to illuminate, to clear, to make nimble and easy, enabling the four to nestle into the circling compliancy of their presencing.

I have offered *ereignen* and *das Ereignis* as an example of Heidegger's creative use of language in reaching old-new thoughts. It is likewise an example of the intellectual and spiritual effort that must be made in order to grasp his German and render it in English. There are similar stories to be told about *wesen* and *Wesen,* which I have often translated in the sense of presencing rather than in reference to essence; or *Bezug,* which in "What Are Poets For?" I have steadily translated as the draft; or *der Riss,* the rift of "Origin" which becomes identified with pain in "Language"; or many other words. Throughout his writings Heidegger is at work shaping his language, that is, his thinking, in the intense, condensed way—*dichtend*—characteristic of the poet, *der Dichter.* Translating him is essentially akin to translating poetry—for it is the poetry of truth and Being that he has been composing all his life.

REFERENCES

The present volume is composed, with Heidegger's consent, of writings from various works, chosen because they fit together to bring out the main drift of his thinking that relates poetry, art, thought, and language to Being and to man's existing as the mortal he is. The following notes indicate the sources.

"The Thinker as Poet"

Aus der Erfahrung des Denkens (Pfullingen: Neske, 1954). Heidegger notes at the end that this was written in 1947.

"The Origin of the Work of Art"

Der Ursprung des Kunstwerkes, Universal-Bibliothek Nr. 8446/47 (Stuttgart: Reclam, 1960). This is a new, slightly revised edition of the essay by the same title that appeared in *Holzwege* (1st ed; Frankfurt am Main: Klostermann, 1950), which itself went through several printings and some changes. Prefacing the Reclam edition Heidegger writes:

The first version of the present treatise was a lecture given on November 13, 1935, to the Kunstwissenschaftliche Gesellschaft at Freiburg i. Br. and which was repeated in January 1936 in Zürich at the invitation of the student body of the university. The book *Holzwege* contains the text of three lectures at the Freies Deutsches Hochstift in Frankfurt a. M. on November 17 and 24 and December 4, 1936. The Epilogue was, in part, written later.

The *Holzwege* text incorporated in this special edition has been

xxiii

newly revised. The Addendum, written in 1956, explains some of the leading words.

The introduction composed by H.-G. Gadamer contains a decisive hint for the reader of my later writings.

This Reclam edition is dedicated to the memory of Theodor Hetzer.

"What Are Poets For?"

"Wozu Dichter?"—another of the essays published in *Holzwege*. Of this, Heidegger writes in the notes for that volume: "The lecture was delivered to a very small group in commemoration of the twentieth anniversary of R. M. Rilke's death (died December 29, 1926). On the textual question cf. Ernst Zinn's study in *Euphorion N. F.,* Vol. 37(1936), pp. 125 ff."

By the way, concerning all the essays in *Holzwege,* Heidegger had the following to say at the end of his notes: "In the intervening time these pieces have been repeatedly revised and, in some places, clarified. The respective plane of reflection and the structure have remained and also, along with that, the changing use of language."

"Building Dwelling Thinking"

"Bauen Wohnen Denken," in *Vorträge und Aufsätze* (Pfullingen: Neske, 1954). In the references at the back of this volume Heidegger says of this essay: "Lecture, given on August 5, 1951, in the course of the *Darmstadt Colloquium II* on 'Man and Space,' printed in the Proceedings of this colloquium, Neue Darmstädter Verlagsanstalt (1952), pp. 72 ff."

"The Thing"

"Das Ding," in *Vorträge und Aufsätze.* Heidegger's account in the references is: "Lecture, given at the Bayerischen Akademie der Schönen Kunste, on June 6, 1950; printed in the *Jahrbuch der Akademie,* Band I, *Gestalt und Gedanke* 1951, pp. 128 ff. (editor, Clemens Graf Podewils)."

"Language"

"Die Sprache," in *Unterwegs zur Sprache* (Pfullingen: Neske, 1959). In this volume's references Heidegger writes: "The lecture was given on October 7, 1950, at Bühlerhöhe in memory of Max Kommerell and was repeated on February 14, 1951 at the Württembergische Bibliotheksgesellschaft in Stuttgart. The lecture, hitherto unpublished, has become known in the form of many transcripts and notes."

". . . Poetically Man Dwells . . ."

". . . dichterisch wohnet der Mensch . . ."—in *Vorträge und Aufsätze*. Heidegger's account: "Lecture, given on October 6th, 1951, at "Bühlerhöhe"; printed in the first number of *Akzente, Zeitschrift für Dichtung* (edited by W. Höllerer and Hans Bender), No. 1, 1954, pp. 57 ff.

THE THINKER AS POET

(Aus der Erfahrung des Denkens)

Way and weighing
Stile and saying
On a single walk are found.

Go bear without halt
Question and default
On your single pathway bound.

When the early morning light quietly
grows above the mountains . . . .

> The world's darkening never reaches
> to the light of Being.

> We are too late for the gods and too
> early for Being. Being's poem,
> just begun, is man.

> To head toward a star—this only.

> To think is to confine yourself to a
> single thought that one day stands
> still like a star in the world's sky.

When the little windwheel outside
the cabin window sings in the
gathering thunderstorm . . . .

>When thought's courage stems from
the bidding of Being, then
destiny's language thrives.

>As soon as we have the thing before
our eyes, and in our hearts an ear
for the word, thinking prospers.

>Few are experienced enough in the
difference between an object of
scholarship and a matter thought.

>If in thinking there were already
adversaries and not mere
opponents, then thinking's case
would be more auspicious.

When through a rent in the rain-clouded
sky a ray of the sun suddenly glides
over the gloom of the meadows . . . .

> We never come to thoughts. They come
>   to us.
>
> That is the proper hour of discourse.
>
> Discourse cheers us to companionable
>   reflection. Such reflection neither
>   parades polemical opinions nor does it
>   tolerate complaisant agreement. The sail
>   of thinking keeps trimmed hard to the
>   wind of the matter.
>
> From such companionship a few perhaps
>   may rise to be journeymen in the
>   craft of thinking. So that one of them,
>   unforeseen, may become a master.

When in early summer lonely narcissi
bloom hidden in the meadow and the
rock-rose gleams under the maple . . . .

   The splendor of the simple.

   Only image formed keeps the vision.
   Yet image formed rests in the poem.

   How could cheerfulness stream
    through us if we wanted to shun
    sadness?

   Pain gives of its healing power
    where we least expect it.

When the wind, shifting quickly, grumbles
in the rafters of the cabin, and the
weather threatens to become nasty . . . .

Three dangers threaten thinking.

The good and thus wholesome
    danger is the nighness of the singing
    poet.

The evil and thus keenest danger is
    thinking itself. It must think
    against itself, which it can only
    seldom do.

The bad and thus muddled danger
    is philosophizing.

When on a summer's day the butterfly
settles on the flower and, wings
closed, sways with it in the
meadow-breeze . . . .

> All our heart's courage is the
> echoing response to the
> first call of Being which
> gathers our thinking into the
> play of the world.

> In thinking all things
> become solitary and slow.

> Patience nurtures magnanimity.

> He who thinks greatly must
> err greatly.

When the mountain brook in night's
stillness tells of its plunging
over the boulders . . . .

The oldest of the old follows behind
    us in our thinking and yet it
    comes to meet us.

That is why thinking holds to the
    coming of what has been, and
    is remembrance.

To be old means: to stop in time at
    that place where the unique
    thought of a thought train has
    swung into its joint.

We may venture the step back out
    of philosophy into the thinking of
    Being as soon as we have grown
    familiar with the provenance of
    thinking.

When in the winter nights snowstorms
tear at the cabin and one morning the
landscape is hushed in its blanket of
snow . . . .

> Thinking's saying would be stilled in
>   its being only by becoming unable
>   to say that which must remain
>   unspoken.
>
> Such inability would bring thinking
>   face to face with its matter.
>
> What is spoken is never, and in no
>   language, what is said.
>
> That a thinking is, ever and suddenly—
>   whose amazement could fathom it?

When the cowbells keep tinkling from
the slopes of the mountain valley
where the herds wander slowly . . . .

> The poetic character of thinking is
> still veiled over.
>
> Where it shows itself, it is for a
> long time like the utopism of
> a half-poetic intellect.
>
> But poetry that thinks is in truth
> the topology of Being.
>
> This topology tells Being the
> whereabouts of its actual
> presence.

When the evening light, slanting into
the woods somewhere, bathes the tree
trunks in gold . . . .

Singing and thinking are the stems
neighbor to poetry.

They grow out of Being and reach into
its truth.

Their relationship makes us think of what
Hölderlin sings of the trees of the
woods:

"And to each other they remain unknown,
So long as they stand, the neighboring
trunks."

Forests spread
Brooks plunge
Rocks persist
Mist diffuses

Meadows wait
Springs well
Winds dwell
Blessing muses

THE ORIGIN OF THE WORK OF ART

THE ORIGIN OF THE WORK OF ART

Origin here means that from and by which something is what it is and as it is. What something is, as it is, we call its essence or nature. The origin of something is the source of its nature. The question concerning the origin of the work of art asks about the source of its nature. On the usual view, the work arises out of and by means of the activity of the artist. But by what and whence is the artist what he is? By the work; for to say that the work does credit to the master means that it is the work that first lets the artist emerge as a master of his art. The artist is the origin of the work. The work is the origin of the artist. Neither is without the other. Nevertheless, neither is the sole support of the other. In themselves and in their interrelations artist and work *are* each of them by virtue of a third thing which is prior to both, namely that which also gives artist and work of art their names—art.

As necessarily as the artist is the origin of the work in a different way than the work is the origin of the artist, so it is equally certain that, in a still different way, art is the origin of both artist and work. But can art be an origin at all? Where and how does art occur? Art—this is nothing more than a word to which nothing real any longer corresponds. It may pass for a collective idea under which we find a place for that which alone is real in art: works and artists. Even if the word art were taken to signify more than a collective notion, what is meant by the word could exist only on the basis of the actuality of works and artists. Or is the converse the case? Do works and artists exist only because art exists as their origin?

Whatever the decision may be, the question of the origin of the work of art becomes a question about the nature of art. Since the question whether and how art in general exists must still remain open, we shall attempt to discover the nature of art in the place where art undoubtedly prevails in a real way. Art is present in the art work. But what and how is a work of art?

What art is should be inferable from the work. What the work of art is we can come to know only from the nature of art. Anyone can easily see that we are moving in a circle. Ordinary understanding demands that this circle be avoided because it violates logic. What art is can be gathered from a comparative examination of actual art works. But how are we to be certain that we are indeed basing such an examination on art works if we do not know beforehand what art is? And the nature of art can no more be arrived at by a derivation from higher concepts than by a collection of characteristics of actual art works. For such a derivation, too, already has in view the characteristics that must suffice to establish that what we take in advance to be an art work is one in fact. But selecting works from among given objects, and deriving concepts from principles, are equally impossible here, and where these procedures are practiced they are a self-deception.

Thus we are compelled to follow the circle. This is neither a makeshift nor a defect. To enter upon this path is the strength of thought, to continue on it is the feast of thought, assuming that thinking is a craft. Not only is the main step from work to art a circle like the step from art to work, but every separate step that we attempt circles in this circle.

In order to discover the nature of the art that really prevails in the work, let us go to the actual work and ask the work what and how it is.

Works of art are familiar to everyone. Architectural and

sculptural works can be seen installed in public places, in churches, and in dwellings. Art works of the most diverse periods and peoples are housed in collections and exhibitions. If we consider the works in their untouched actuality and do not deceive ourselves, the result is that the works are as naturally present as are things. The picture hangs on the wall like a rifle or a hat. A painting, e.g., the one by Van Gogh that represents a pair of peasant shoes, travels from one exhibition to another. Works of art are shipped like coal from the Ruhr and logs from the Black Forest. During the First World War Hölderlin's hymns were packed in the soldier's knapsack together with cleaning gear. Beethoven's quartets lie in the storerooms of the publishing house like potatoes in a cellar.

All works have this thingly character. What would they be without it? But perhaps this rather crude and external view of the work is objectionable to us. Shippers or charwomen in museums may operate with such conceptions of the work of art. We, however, have to take works as they are encountered by those who experience and enjoy them. But even the much-vaunted aesthetic experience cannot get around the thingly aspect of the art work. There is something stony in a work of architecture, wooden in a carving, colored in a painting, spoken in a linguistic work, sonorous in a musical composition. The thingly element is so irremovably present in the art work that we are compelled rather to say conversely that the architectural work is in stone, the carving is in wood, the painting in color, the linguistic work in speech, the musical composition in sound. "Obviously," it will be replied. No doubt. But what is this self-evident thingly element in the work of art?

Presumably it becomes superfluous and confusing to inquire into this feature, since the art work is something else over and above the thingly element. This something else in the work constitutes its artistic nature. The art work is, to be sure, a thing that is made, but it says something other than the mere thing itself is, *allo agoreuei*. The work makes public something other than itself; it manifests something other; it is an allegory. In the work of art something other is brought together with the thing that is made. To bring together is, in Greek, *sumballein*. The work is a symbol.

Allegory and symbol provide the conceptual frame within whose channel of vision the art work has for a long time been characterized. But this one element in a work that manifests another, this one element that joins with another, is the thingly feature in the art work. It seems almost as though the thingly element in the art work is like the substructure into and upon which the other, authentic element is built. And is it not this thingly feature in the work that the artist really makes by his handicraft?

Our aim is to arrive at the immediate and full reality of the work of art, for only in this way shall we discover real art also within it. Hence we must first bring to view the thingly element of the work. To this end it is necessary that we should know with sufficient clarity what a thing is. Only then can we say whether the art work is a thing, but a thing to which something else adheres; only then can we decide whether the work is at bottom something else and not a thing at all.

Thing and Work

What in truth is the thing, so far as it is a thing? When we inquire in this way, our aim is to come to know the thing-being (thingness) of the thing. The point is to discover the thingly character of the thing. To this end we have to be acquainted with the sphere to which all those entities belong which we have long called by the name of thing.

The stone in the road is a thing, as is the clod in the field. A jug is a thing, as is the well beside the road. But what about the milk in the jug and the water in the well? These too are things if the cloud in the sky and the thistle in the field, the leaf in the autumn breeze and the hawk over the wood, are rightly called by the name of thing. All these must indeed be called things, if the name is applied even to that which does not, like those just enumerated, show itself, i.e., that which does not appear. According to Kant, the whole of the world, for example, and even God himself, is a thing of this sort, a thing that does not itself appear, namely, a "thing-in-itself." In the language of philosophy both things-in-themselves and things that appear, all beings that in any way are, are called things.

Airplanes and radio sets are nowadays among the things closest to us, but when we have ultimate things in mind we think of something altogether different. Death and judgment—these are ultimate things. On the whole the word "thing" here designates whatever is not simply nothing. In this sense the work of art is also a thing, so far as it is not simply nothing. Yet this concept is of no use to us, at least immediately, in our attempt to delimit entities that have the mode of being of a thing, as against those having the mode of being of a work. And besides, we hesitate to call God a thing. In the same way we hesitate to consider the peasant in the field, the stoker at the boiler, the teacher in the school as things. A man is not a thing. It is true that we speak of a young girl who is faced with a task too difficult for her as being a young thing, still too young for it, but only because we feel that being human is in a certain way missing here and think that instead we have to do here with the factor that constitutes the thingly character of things. We hesitate even to call the deer in the forest clearing, the beetle in the grass, the blade of grass a thing. We would sooner think of a hammer as a thing, or a shoe, or an ax, or a clock. But even these are not mere things. Only a stone, a clod of earth, a piece of wood are for us such mere things. Lifeless beings of nature and objects of use. Natural things and utensils are the things commonly so called.

We thus see ourselves brought back from the widest domain, within which everything is a thing (thing = *res* = *ens* = an entity), including even the highest and last things, to the narrow precinct of mere things. "Mere" here means, first, the pure thing, which is simply a thing and nothing more; but then, at the same time, it means that which is only a thing, in an almost pejorative sense. It is mere things, excluding even use-objects, that count as things in the strict sense. What does the thingly character of these things, then, consist in? It is in reference to these that the thingness of things must be determinable. This determination enables us to characterize what it is that is thingly as such. Thus prepared, we are able to characterize the almost palpable reality of works, in which something else inheres.

Now it passes for a known fact that as far back as antiquity, no sooner was the question raised as to what entities are in general, than things in their thingness thrust themselves into prominence again and again as the standard type of beings. Consequently we are bound to meet with the definition of the thingness of things already in the traditional interpretations of beings. We thus need only to ascertain explicitly this traditional knowledge of the thing, to be relieved of the tedious labor of making our own search for the thingly character of the thing. The answers to the question "What is the thing?" are so familiar that we no longer sense anything questionable behind them.

The interpretations of the thingness of the thing which, predominant in the course of Western thought, have long become self-evident and are now in everyday use, may be reduced to three.

This block of granite, for example, is a mere thing. It is hard, heavy, extended, bulky, shapeless, rough, colored, partly dull, partly shiny. We can take note of all these features in the stone. Thus we acknowledge its characteristics. But still, the traits signify something proper to the stone itself. They are its properties. The thing has them. The thing? What are we thinking of when we now have the thing in mind? Obviously a thing is not merely an aggregate of traits, nor an accumulation of properties by which that aggregate arises. A thing, as everyone thinks he knows, is that around which the properties have assembled. We speak in this connection of the core of things. The Greeks are supposed to have called it *to hupokeimenon.* For them, this core of the thing was something lying at the ground of the thing, something always already there. The characteristics, however, are called *ta sumbebekota,* that which has always turned up already along with the given core and occurs along with it.

These designations are no arbitrary names. Something that lies beyond the purview of this essay speaks in them, the basic Greek experience of the Being of beings in the sense of presence. It is by these determinations, however, that the interpretation of the thingness of the thing is established which henceforth becomes standard, and the Western interpretation of the Being of beings stabilized. The process begins with the appropriation of Greek words by Roman-Latin thought. *Hupokeimenon* becomes *subiectum; hupostasis* becomes *substantia; sumbebekos* becomes *accidens.* However, this translation of Greek names into Latin is in no way the innocent process it is considered to this day. Beneath the seemingly literal and thus faithful translation there is concealed, rather, a *trans*lation of Greek experience into a different way of thinking. *Roman thought takes over the Greek words without a corresponding, equally authentic experience of what they say, without the Greek word.* The rootlessness of Western thought begins with this translation.

According to current opinion, this definition of the thingness of the thing as the substance with its accidents seems to correspond to our natural outlook on things. No wonder that the current attitude toward things—our way of addressing ourselves to things and speaking about them—has adapted itself to this common view of the thing. A simple propositional statement consists of the subject, which is the Latin translation, hence already a reinterpretation, of *hupokeimenon* and the predicate, in which the thing's traits are stated of it. Who would have the temerity to assail these simple fundamental relations between thing and statement, between sentence structure and thing-structure? Nevertheless we must ask: Is the structure of a simple propositional statement (the combination of subject and predicate) the mirror image of the structure of the thing (of the union of substance with accidents)? Or could it be that even the structure of the thing as thus envisaged is a projection of the framework of the sentence?

What could be more obvious than that man transposes his propositional way of understanding things into the structure of the thing itself? Yet this view, seemingly critical yet actually rash and ill-considered, would have to explain first how such a transposition of propositional structure into the thing is supposed to be possible without the thing having already become visible. The question which comes first and functions as the standard, proposition structure or thing-structure remains to this hour undecided. It even remains doubtful whether in this form the question is at all decidable.

Actually, the sentence structure does not provide the standard for the pattern of thing-structure, nor is the latter simply mirrored in the former. Both sentence and thing-structure derive, in their typical form and their possible mutual relationship, from a common and more original source. In any case this first interpretation of the thingness of the thing, the thing as bearer of its characteristic traits, despite its currency, is not as natural as it appears to be. What seems natural to us is probably just something familiar in a long tradition that has forgotten the unfamiliar source from which it arose. And yet this unfamiliar source once struck man as strange and caused him to think and to wonder.

Our reliance on the current interpretation of the thing is only seemingly well founded. But in addition this thing-concept (the thing as bearer of its characteristics) holds not only of the mere thing in its strict sense, but also of any being whatsoever. Hence it cannot be used to set apart thingly beings from non-thingly beings. Yet even before all reflection, attentive dwelling within the sphere of things already tells us that this thing-concept does not hit upon the thingly element of the thing, its independent and self-contained character. Occasionally we still have the feeling that violence has long been done to the thingly element of things and that thought has played a part in this violence, for which reason people disavow thought instead of taking pains to make it more thoughtful. But in defining the nature of the thing, what is the use of a feeling, however certain, if thought alone has the right to speak here? Perhaps however what we call feeling or mood, here and in similar instances, is more reasonable—that is, more intelligently perceptive—because more open to Being than all that reason which, having meanwhile become *ratio,* was misinterpreted as being rational. The hankering after the irrational, as abortive offspring of the unthought rational, therewith performed a curious service. To be sure, the current thing-concept always fits each thing. Nevertheless it does not lay hold of the thing as it is in its own being, but makes an assault upon it.

Can such an assault perhaps be avoided—and how? Only, certainly, by granting the thing, as it were, a free field to display its thingly character directly. Everything that might interpose itself between the thing and us in apprehending and talking about it must first be set aside. Only then do we yield ourselves to the undisguised presence of the thing. But we do not need first to call or arrange for this situation in which we let things encounter us without mediation. The situation always prevails. In what the senses of sight, hearing, and touch convey, in the sensations of color, sound, roughness, hardness, things move us bodily, in the literal meaning of the word. The thing is the *aistheton,* that which is perceptible by sensations in the senses belonging to sensibility. Hence the concept later becomes a commonplace according to which a thing is nothing but the unity of a manifold of what is given in the senses. Whether this unity is conceived as sum or as totality or as form alters nothing in the standard character of this thing-concept.

Now this interpretation of the thingness of the thing is as correct and demonstrable in every case as the previous one. This already suffices to cast doubt on its truth. If we consider moreover what we are searching for, the thingly character of the thing, then this thing-concept again leaves us at a loss. We never really first perceive a throng of sensations, e.g., tones and noises, in the appearance of things—as this thing-concept alleges; rather we hear the storm whistling in the chimney, we hear the three-motored plane, we hear the Mercedes in immediate distinction from the Volkswagen. Much closer to us than all sensations are the things themselves. We hear the door shut in the house and never hear acoustical sensations or even mere sounds. In order to hear a bare sound we have to listen away from things, divert our ear from them, i.e., listen abstractly.

In the thing-concept just mentioned there is not so much an assault upon the thing as rather an inordinate attempt to bring it into the greatest possible proximity to us. But a thing never reaches that position as long as we assign as its thingly feature what is perceived by the senses. Whereas the first interpretation keeps the thing at arm's length from us, as it were, and sets it too far off, the second makes it press too hard upon us. In both interpretations the thing vanishes. It is therefore necessary to avoid the exaggerations of both. The thing itself must be allowed to remain in its self-containment. It must be accepted in its own constancy. This the third interpretation seems to do, which is just as old as the first two.

That which gives things their constancy and pith but is also at the same time the source of their particular mode of sensuous pressure—colored, resonant, hard, massive—is the matter in things. In this analysis of the thing as matter (*hule*), form (*morphe*) is already coposited. What is constant in a thing, its consistency, lies in the fact that matter stands together with a form. The thing is formed matter. This interpretation appeals to the immediate view with which the thing solicits us by its looks (*eidos*). In this synthesis of matter and form a thing-concept has finally been found which applies equally to things of nature and to use-objects.

This concept puts us in a position to answer the question concerning the thingly element in the work of art. The thingly element is manifestly the matter of which it consists. Matter is the substrate and field for the artist's formative action. But we could have advanced this obvious and well-known definition of the thingly element at the very outset. Why do we make a detour through other current thing-concepts? Because we also mistrust this concept of the thing, which represents it as formed matter.

But is not precisely this pair of concepts, matter-form, usually employed in the domain in which we are supposed to be moving? To be sure. The distinction of matter and form is *the conceptual schema which is used, in the greatest variety of ways, quite generally for all art theory and aesthetics.* This incontestable fact, however, proves neither that the distinction of matter and form is adequately founded, nor that it belongs originally to the domain of art and the art work. Moreover, the range of application of this pair of concepts has long extended far beyond the field of aesthetics. Form and content are the most hackneyed concepts under which anything and everything may be subsumed. And if form is correlated with the rational and matter with the irrational; if the rational is taken to be the logical and the irrational the alogical; if in addition the subject-object relation is coupled with the conceptual pair form-matter; then representation has at its command a conceptual machinery that nothing is capable of withstanding.

If, however, it is thus with the distinction between matter and form, how then shall we make use of it to lay hold of the particular domain of mere things by contrast with all other entities? But perhaps this characterization in terms of matter and form would recover its defining power if only we reversed the process of expanding and emptying these concepts. Certainly, but this presupposes that we know in what sphere of beings they realize their true defining power. That this is the domain of mere things is so far only an assumption. Reference to the copious use made of this conceptual framework in aesthetics might sooner lead to the idea that matter and form are specifications stemming from the nature of the art work and were in the first place transferred from it back to the thing. Where does the matter-form structure have its origin—in the thingly character of the thing or in the workly character of the art work?

The self-contained block of granite is something material in a definite if unshapely form. Form means here the distribution and arrangement of the material parts in spatial locations, resulting in a particular shape, namely that of a block. But a jug, an ax, a shoe are also matter occurring in a form. Form as shape is not the consequence here of a prior distribution of the matter. The form, on the contrary, determines the arrangement of the matter. Even more, it prescribes in each case the kind and selection of the matter—impermeable for a jug, sufficiently hard for an ax, firm yet flexible for shoes. The interfusion of form and matter prevailing here is, moreover, controlled beforehand by the purposes served by jug, ax, shoes. Such usefulness is never assigned or added on afterward to a being of the type of a jug, ax, or pair of shoes. But neither is it something that floats somewhere above it as an end.

Usefulness is the basic feature from which this entity regards us, that is, flashes at us and thereby is present and thus is this entity. Both the formative act and the choice of material—a choice given with the act—and therewith the dominance of the conjunction of matter and form, are all grounded in such usefulness. A being that falls under usefulness is always the product of a process of making. It is made as a piece of equipment for something. As determinations of beings, accordingly, matter and form have their proper place in the essential nature of equipment. This name designates what is produced expressly for employment and use. Matter and form are in no case original determinations of the thingness of the mere thing.

A piece of equipment, a pair of shoes for instance, when finished, is also self-contained like the mere thing, but it does not have the character of having taken shape by itself like the granite boulder. On the other hand, equipment displays an affinity with the art work insofar as it is something produced by the human hand. However, by its self-sufficient presence the work of art is similar rather to the mere thing which has taken shape by itself and is self-contained. Nevertheless we do not count such works among mere things. As a rule it is the use-objects around us that are the nearest and authentic things. Thus the piece of equipment is half thing, because characterized by thingliness, and yet it is something more; at the same time it is half art work and yet something less, because lacking the self-sufficiency of the art work. Equipment has a peculiar position intermediate between thing and work, assuming that such a calculated ordering of them is permissible.

The matter-form structure, however, by which the being of a piece of equipment is first determined, readily presents itself as the immediately intelligible constitution of every entity, because here man himself as maker participates in the way in which the piece of equipment comes into being. Because equipment takes an intermediate place between mere thing and work, the suggestion is that nonequipmental beings—things and works and ultimately everything that is—are to be comprehended with the help of the being of equipment (the matter-form structure).

The inclination to treat the matter-form structure as *the* constitution of every entity receives a yet additional impulse from the fact that on the basis of a religious faith, namely, the biblical faith, the totality of all beings is represented in advance as something created, which here means made. The philosophy of this faith can of course assure us that all of God's creative work is to be thought of as different from the action of a craftsman. Nevertheless, if at the same time or even beforehand, in accordance with a presumed predetermination of Thomistic philosophy for interpreting the Bible, the *ens creatum* is conceived as a unity of *materia* and *forma,* then faith is expounded by way of a philosophy whose truth lies in an unconcealedness of beings which differs in kind from the world believed in by faith.

The idea of creation, grounded in faith, can lose its guiding power of knowledge of beings as a whole. But the theological interpretation of all beings, the view of the world in terms of matter and form borrowed from an alien philosophy, having once been instituted, can still remain a force. This happens in the transition from the Middle Ages to modern times. The metaphysics of the modern period rests on the form-matter structure devised in the medieval period, which itself merely recalls in its words the buried natures of *eidos* and *hule.* Thus the interpretation of "thing" by means of matter and form, whether it remains medieval or becomes Kantian-transcendental, has become current and self-evident. But for that reason, no less than the other interpretations mentioned of the thingness of the thing, it is an encroachment upon the thing-being of the thing.

The situation stands revealed as soon as we speak of things in the strict sense as mere things. The "mere," after all, means the removal of the character of usefulness and of being made. The mere thing is a sort of equipment, albeit equipment denuded of its equipmental being. Thing-being consists in what is then left over. But this remnant is not actually defined in its ontological character. It remains doubtful whether the thingly character comes to view at all in the process of stripping off everything equipmental. Thus the third mode of interpretation of the thing, that which follows the lead of the matter-form structure, also turns out to be an assault upon the thing.

These three modes of defining thingness conceive of the thing as a bearer of traits, as the unity of a manifold of sensations, as formed matter. In the course of the history of truth about beings, the interpretations mentioned have also entered into combinations, a matter we may now pass over. In such combination they have further strengthened their innate tendency to expand so as to apply in similar way to thing, to equipment, and to work. Thus they give rise to a mode of thought by which we think not only about thing, equipment, and work but about all beings in general. This long-familiar mode of thought pre-conceives all immediate experience of beings. The preconception shackles reflection on the being of any given entity. Thus it comes about that prevailing thing-concepts obstruct the way toward the thingly character of the thing as well as toward the equipmental character of equipment, and all the more toward the workly character of the work.

This fact is the reason why it is necessary to know about these thing-concepts, in order thereby to take heed of their derivation and their boundless presumption, but also of their semblance of self-evidence. This knowledge becomes all the more necessary when we risk the attempt to bring to view and express in words the thingly character of the thing, the equipmental character of equipment, and the workly character of the work. To this end, however, only one element is needful: to keep at a distance all the preconceptions and assaults of the above modes of thought, to leave the thing to rest in its own self, for instance, in its thing-being. What seems easier than to let a being be just the being that it is? Or does this turn out to be the most difficult of tasks, particularly if such an intention —to let a being be as it is—represents the opposite of the in-difference that simply turns its back upon the being itself in favor of an unexamined concept of being? We ought to turn toward the being, think about it in regard to its being, but by means of this thinking at the same time let it rest upon itself in its very own being.

This exertion of thought seems to meet with its greatest resistance in defining the thingness of the thing; for where else could the cause lie of the failure of the efforts mentioned? The unpretentious thing evades thought most stubbornly. Or can it be that this self-refusal of the mere thing, this self-contained independence, belongs precisely to the nature of the thing? Must not this strange and uncommunicative feature of the nature of the thing become intimately familiar to thought that tries to think the thing? If so, then we should not force our way to its thingly character.

That the thingness of the thing is particularly difficult to express and only seldom expressible is infallibly documented by the history of its interpretation indicated above. This history coincides with the destiny in accordance with which Western thought has hitherto thought the Being of beings. However, not only do we now establish this point; at the same time we discover a clue in this history. Is it an accident that in the interpretation of the thing the view that takes matter and form as guide attains to special dominance? This definition of the thing derives from an interpretation of the equipmental being of equipment. And equipment, having come into being through human making, is particularly familiar to human thinking. At the same time, this familiar being has a peculiar intermediate position between thing and work. We shall follow this clue and search first for the equipmental character of equipment. Perhaps this will suggest something to us about the thingly character of the thing and the workly character of the work. We must only avoid making thing and work prematurely into subspecies of equipment. We are disregarding the possibility, however, that differences relating to the history of Being may yet also be present in the way equipment *is*.

But what path leads to the equipmental quality of equipment? How shall we discover what a piece of equipment truly is? The procedure necessary at present must plainly avoid any attempts that again immediately entail the encroachments of the usual interpretations. We are most easily insured against this if we simply describe some equipment without any philosophical theory.

We choose as example a common sort of equipment—a pair of peasant shoes. We do not even need to exhibit actual pieces of this sort of useful article in order to describe them. Everyone is acquainted with them. But since it is a matter here of direct description, it may be well to facilitate the visual realization of them. For this purpose a pictorial representation suffices. We shall choose a well-known painting by Van Gogh, who painted such shoes several times. But what is there to see here? Everyone knows what shoes consist of. If they are not wooden or bast shoes, there will be leather soles and uppers, joined together by thread and nails. Such gear serves to clothe the feet. Depending on the use to which the shoes are to be put, whether for work in the field or for dancing, matter and form will differ.

Such statements, no doubt correct, only explicate what we already know. The equipmental quality of equipment consists in its usefulness. But what about this usefulness itself? In conceiving it, do we already conceive along with it the equipmental character of equipment? In order to succeed in doing this, must we not look out for useful equipment in its use? The peasant woman wears her shoes in the field. Only here are they what they are. They are all the more genuinely so, the less the peasant woman thinks about the shoes while she is at work, or looks at them at all, or is even aware of them. She stands and walks in them. That is how shoes actually serve. It is in this process of the use of equipment that we must actually encounter the character of equipment.

As long as we only imagine a pair of shoes in general, or simply look at the empty, unused shoes as they merely stand there in the picture, we shall never discover what the equipmental being of the equipment in truth is. From Van Gogh's painting we cannot even tell where these shoes stand. There is nothing surrounding this pair of peasant shoes in or to which they might belong—only an undefined space. There are not even clods of soil from the field or the field-path sticking to them, which would at least hint at their use. A pair of peasant shoes and nothing more. And yet—

From the dark opening of the worn insides of the shoes the

toilsome tread of the worker stares forth. In the stiffly rugged heaviness of the shoes there is the accumulated tenacity of her slow trudge through the far-spreading and ever-uniform furrows of the field swept by a raw wind. On the leather lie the dampness and richness of the soil. Under the soles slides the loneliness of the field-path as evening falls. In the shoes vibrates the silent call of the earth, its quiet gift of the ripening grain and its unexplained self-refusal in the fallow desolation of the wintry field. This equipment is pervaded by uncomplaining anxiety as to the certainty of bread, the wordless joy of having once more withstood want, the trembling before the impending childbed and shivering at the surrounding menace of death. This equipment belongs to the *earth,* and it is protected in the *world* of the peasant woman. From out of this protected belonging the equipment itself rises to its resting-within-itself.

But perhaps it is only in the picture that we notice all this about the shoes. The peasant woman, on the other hand, simply wears them. If only this simple wearing were so simple. When she takes off her shoes late in the evening, in deep but healthy fatigue, and reaches out for them again in the still dim dawn, or passes them by on the day of rest, she knows all this without noticing or reflecting. The equipmental quality of the equipment consists indeed in its usefulness. But this usefulness itself rests in the abundance of an essential being of the equipment. We call it reliability. By virtue of this reliability the peasant woman is made privy to the silent call of the earth; by virtue of the reliability of the equipment she is sure of her world. World and earth exist for her, and for those who are with her in her mode of being, only thus—in the equipment. We say "only" and therewith fall into error; for the reliability of the equipment first gives to the simple world its security and assures to the earth the freedom of its steady thrust.

The equipmental being of equipment, reliability, keeps gathered within itself all things according to their manner and extent. The usefulness of equipment is nevertheless only the essential consequence of reliability. The former vibrates in the latter and would be nothing without it. A single piece of equipment is worn out and used up; but at the same time the use itself also falls into disuse, wears away, and becomes usual. Thus equipmentality wastes away, sinks into mere stuff. In such wasting, reliability vanishes. This dwindling, however, to which use-things owe their boringly obtrusive usualness, is only one more testimony to the original nature of equipmental being. The worn-out usualness of the equipment then obtrudes itself as the sole mode of being, apparently peculiar to it exclusively. Only blank usefulness now remains visible. It awakens the impression that the origin of equipment lies in a mere fabricating that impresses a form upon some matter. Nevertheless, in its genuinely equipmental being, equipment stems from a more distant source. Matter and form and their distinction have a deeper origin.

The repose of equipment resting within itself consists in its reliability. Only in this reliability do we discern what equipment in truth is. But we still know nothing of what we first sought: the thing's thingly character. And we know nothing at all of what we really and solely seek: the workly character of the work in the sense of the work of art.

Or have we already learned something unwittingly, in passing so to speak, about the work-being of the work?

The equipmental quality of equipment was discovered. But how? Not by a description and explanation of a pair of shoes actually present; not by a report about the process of making shoes; and also not by the observation of the actual use of shoes occurring here and there; but only by bringing ourselves before Van Gogh's painting. This painting spoke. In the vicinity of the work we were suddenly somewhere else than we usually tend to be.

The art work let us know what shoes are in truth. It would be the worst self-deception to think that our description, as a subjective action, had first depicted everything thus and then projected it into the painting. If anything is questionable here, it is rather that we experienced too little in the neighborhood of the work and that we expressed the experience too crudely and too literally. But above all, the work did not, as it might seem at first, serve merely for a better visualizing of what a piece of equipment is. Rather, the equipmentality of equipment first genuinely arrives at its appearance through the work and only in the work.

What happens here? What is at work in the work? Van Gogh's painting is the disclosure of what the equipment, the pair of peasant shoes, *is* in truth. This entity emerges into the unconcealedness of its being. The Greeks called the unconcealedness of beings *aletheia*. We say "truth" and think little enough in using this word. If there occurs in the work a disclosure of a particular being, disclosing what and how it is, then there is here an occurring, a happening of truth at work.

In the work of art the truth of an entity has set itself to work. "To set" means here: to bring to a stand. Some particular entity, a pair of peasant shoes, comes in the work to stand in the light of its being. The being of the being comes into the steadiness of its shining.

The nature of art would then be this: the truth of beings setting itself to work. But until now art presumably has had to do with the beautiful and beauty, and not with truth. The arts that produce such works are called the beautiful or fine arts, in contrast with the applied or industrial arts that manufacture equipment. In fine art the art itself is not beautiful, but is called so because it produces the beautiful. Truth, in contrast, belongs to logic. Beauty, however, is reserved for aesthetics.

But perhaps the proposition that art is truth setting itself to work intends to revive the fortunately obsolete view that art is an imitation and depiction of reality? The reproduction of what exists requires, to be sure, agreement with the actual being, adaptation to it; the Middle Ages called it *adaequatio;* Aristotle already spoke of *homoiosis*. Agreement with what *is* has long been taken to be the essence of truth. But then, is it our opinion that this painting by Van Gogh depicts a pair of actually existing peasant shoes, and is a work of art because it does so successfully? Is it our opinion that the painting draws a likeness from something actual and transposes it into a product of artistic——production? By no means.

The work, therefore, is not the reproduction of some particular entity that happens to be present at any given time; it is, on the contrary, the reproduction of the thing's general essence. But then where and how is this general essence, so that art works are able to agree with it? With what nature of what thing should a Greek temple agree? Who could maintain the impossible view that the Idea of Temple is represented in the building? And yet, truth is set to work in such a work, if it is a work. Or let us think of Hölderlin's hymn, "The Rhine." What is pregiven to the poet, and how is it given, so that it can then be regiven in the poem? And if in the case of this hymn and similar poems the idea of a copy-relation between something already actual and the art work clearly fails, the view that the work is a copy is confirmed in the best possible way by a work of the kind presented in C. F. Meyer's poem "Roman Fountain."

Roman Fountain

> The jet ascends and falling fills
> The marble basin circling round;
> This, veiling itself over, spills
> Into a second basin's ground.
> The second in such plenty lives,
> Its bubbling flood a third invests,
> And each at once receives and gives
> And streams and rests.

This is neither a poetic painting of a fountain actually present nor a reproduction of the general essence of a Roman fountain.

Yet truth is put into the work. What truth is happening in the work? Can truth happen at all and thus be historical? Yet truth, people say, is something timeless and supertemporal.

We seek the reality of the art work in order to find there the art prevailing within it. The thingly substructure is what proved to be the most immediate reality in the work. But to comprehend this thingly feature the traditional thing-concepts are not adequate; for they themselves fail to grasp the nature of the thing. The currently predominant thing-concept, thing as formed matter, is not even derived from the nature of the thing but from the nature of equipment. It also turned out that equipmental being generally has long since occupied a peculiar preeminence in the interpretation of beings. This preeminence of equipmentality, which however did not actually come to mind, suggested that we pose the question of equipment anew while avoiding the current interpretations.

We allowed a work to tell us what equipment is. By this means, almost clandestinely, it came to light what is at work in the work: the disclosure of the particular being in its being, the happening of truth. If, however, the reality of the work can be defined solely by means of what is at work in the work, then what about our intention to seek out the real art work in its reality? As long as we supposed that the reality of the work lay primarily in its thingly substructure we were going astray. We are now confronted by a remarkable result of our considerations —if it still deserves to be called a result at all. Two points become clear:

First: the dominant thing-concepts are inadequate as means of grasping the thingly aspect of the work.

Second: what we tried to treat as the most immediate reality of the work, its thingly substructure, does not belong to the work in that way at all.

As soon as we look for such a thingly substructure in the work, we have unwittingly taken the work as equipment, to which we then also ascribe a superstructure supposed to contain its artistic quality. But the work is not a piece of equipment

that is fitted out in addition with an aesthetic value that adheres to it. The work is no more anything of the kind than the
bare thing is a piece of equipment that merely lacks the specific
equipmental characteristics of usefulness and being made.

Our formulation of the question of the work has been shaken
because we asked, not about the work but half about a thing
and half about equipment. Still, this formulation of the question
was not first developed by us. It is the formulation native to
aesthetics. The way in which aesthetics views the art work
from the outset is dominated by the traditional interpretation
of all beings. But the shaking of this accustomed formulation
is not the essential point. What matters is a first opening of our
vision to the fact that what is workly in the work, equipmental
in equipment, and thingly in the thing comes closer to us only
when we think the Being of beings. To this end it is necessary
beforehand that the barriers of our preconceptions fall away
and that the current pseudo concepts be set aside. That is why
we had to take this detour. But it brings us directly to a road
that may lead to a determination of the thingly feature in the
work. The thingly feature in the work should not be denied;
but if it belongs admittedly to the work-being of the work, it
must be conceived by way of the work's workly nature. If this
is so, then the road toward the determination of the thingly
reality of the work leads not from thing to work but from work
to thing.

The art work opens up in its own way the Being of beings.
This opening up, i.e., this deconcealing, i.e., the truth of beings, happens in the work. In the art work, the truth of what is
has set itself to work. Art is truth setting itself to work. What
is truth itself, that it sometimes comes to pass as art? What is
this setting-itself-to-work?

The Work and Truth

The origin of the art work is art. But what is art? Art is real
in the art work. Hence we first seek the reality of the work. In
what does it consist? Art works universally display a thingly

character, albeit in a wholly distinct way. The attempt to interpret this thing-character of the work with the aid of the usual thing-concepts failed—not only because these concepts do not lay hold of the thingly feature, but because, in raising the question of its thingly substructure, we force the work into a preconceived framework by which we obstruct our own access to the work-being of the work. Nothing can be discovered about the thingly aspect of the work so long as the pure self-subsistence of the work has not distinctly displayed itself.

Yet is the work ever in itself accessible? To gain access to the work, it would be necessary to remove it from all relations to something other than itself, in order to let it stand on its own for itself alone. But the artist's most peculiar intention already aims in this direction. The work is to be released by him to its pure self-subsistence. It is precisely in great art—and only such art is under consideration here—that the artist remains inconsequential as compared with the work, almost like a passageway that destroys itself in the creative process for the work to emerge.

Well, then, the works themselves stand and hang in collections and exhibitions. But are they here in themselves as the works they themselves are, or are they not rather here as objects of the art industry? Works are made available for public and private art appreciation. Official agencies assume the care and maintenance of works. Connoisseurs and critics busy themselves with them. Art dealers supply the market. Art-historical study makes the works the objects of a science. Yet in all this busy activity do we encounter the work itself?

The Aegina sculptures in the Munich collection, Sophocles' *Antigone* in the best critical edition, are, as the works they are, torn out of their own native sphere. However high their quality and power of impression, however good their state of preservation, however certain their interpretation, placing them in a collection has withdrawn them from their own world. But even when we make an effort to cancel or avoid such displacement of works—when, for instance, we visit the temple in Paestum at its own site or the Bamberg cathedral on its own square—the world of the work that stands there has perished.

World-withdrawal and world-decay can never be undone. The works are no longer the same as they once were. It is they themselves, to be sure, that we encounter there, but they themselves are gone by. As bygone works they stand over against us in the realm of tradition and conservation. Henceforth they remain merely such objects. Their standing before us is still indeed a consequence of, but no longer the same as, their former self-subsistence. This self-subsistence has fled from them. The whole art industry, even if carried to the extreme and exercised in every way for the sake of works themselves, extends only to the object-being of the works. But this does not constitute their work-being.

But does the work still remain a work if it stands outside all relations? Is it not essential for the work to stand in relations? Yes, of course—except that it remains to ask in what relations it stands.

Where does a work belong? The work belongs, as work, uniquely within the realm that is opened up by itself. For the work-being of the work is present in, and only in, such opening up. We said that in the work there was a happening of truth at work. The reference to Van Gogh's picture tried to point to this happening. With regard to it there arose the question as to what truth is and how truth can happen.

We now ask the question of truth with a view to the work. But in order to become more familiar with what the question involves, it is necessary to make visible once more the happening of truth in the work. For this attempt let us deliberately select a work that cannot be ranked as representational art.

A building, a Greek temple, portrays nothing. It simply stands there in the middle of the rock-cleft valley. The building encloses the figure of the god, and in this concealment lets it stand out into the holy precinct through the open portico. By means of the temple, the god is present in the temple. This presence of the god is in itself the extension and delimitation of the precinct as a holy precinct. The temple and its precinct, however, do not fade away into the indefinite. It is the temple-work that first fits together and at the same time gathers around itself the unity of those paths and relations in which birth and death, disaster and blessing, victory and disgrace, endurance and decline acquire the shape of destiny for human being. The all-governing expanse of this open relational context is the world of this historical people. Only from and in this expanse does the nation first return to itself for the fulfillment of its vocation.

Standing there, the building rests on the rocky ground. This resting of the work draws up out of the rock the mystery of that rock's clumsy yet spontaneous support. Standing there, the building holds its ground against the storm raging above it and so first makes the storm itself manifest in its violence. The luster and gleam of the stone, though itself apparently glowing only by the grace of the sun, yet first brings to light the light of the day, the breadth of the sky, the darkness of the night. The temple's firm towering makes visible the invisible space of air. The steadfastness of the work contrasts with the surge of the surf, and its own repose brings out the raging of the sea. Tree and grass, eagle and bull, snake and cricket first enter into their distinctive shapes and thus come to appear as what they are. The Greeks early called this emerging and rising in itself and in all things *phusis*. It clears and illuminates, also, that on which and in which man bases his dwelling. We call this ground the *earth*. What this word says is not to be associated with the idea of a mass of matter deposited somewhere, or with the merely astronomical idea of a planet. Earth is that whence the arising brings back and shelters everything that arises without violation. In the things that arise, earth is present as the sheltering agent.

The temple-work, standing there, opens up a world and at the same time sets this world back again on earth, which itself only thus emerges as native ground. But men and animals, plants and things, are never present and familiar as unchangeable objects, only to represent incidentally also a fitting environment for the temple, which one fine day is added to what is already there. We shall get closer to what *is,* rather, if we think of all this in reverse order, assuming of course that we have, to begin with, an eye for how differently everything then faces us. Mere reversing, done for its own sake, reveals nothing.

The temple, in its standing there, first gives to things their look and to men their outlook on themselves. This view remains open as long as the work is a work, as long as the god has not fled from it. It is the same with the sculpture of the god, votive offering of the victor in the athletic games. It is not a portrait whose purpose is to make it easier to realize how the god looks; rather, it is a work that lets the god himself be present and thus *is* the god himself. The same holds for the linguistic work. In the tragedy nothing is staged or displayed theatrically, but the battle of the new gods against the old is being fought. The linguistic work, originating in the speech of the people, does not refer to this battle; it transforms the people's saying so that now every living word fights the battle and puts up for decision what is holy and what unholy, what great and what small, what brave and what cowardly, what lofty and what flighty, what master and what slave (cf. Heraclitus, Fragment 53).

In what, then, does the work-being of the work consist? Keeping steadily in view the points just crudely enough indicated, two essential features of the work may for the moment be brought out more distinctly. We set out here, from the long familiar foreground of the work's being, the thingly character which gives support to our customary attitude toward the work.

When a work is brought into a collection or placed in an exhibition we say also that it is "set up." But this setting up differs essentially from setting up in the sense of erecting a building, raising a statue, presenting a tragedy at a holy festival. Such setting up is erecting in the sense of dedication and praise. Here "setting up" no longer means a bare placing. To dedicate means to consecrate, in the sense that in setting up the work the holy is opened up as holy and the god is invoked into the openness of his presence. Praise belongs to dedication as doing honor to the dignity and splendor of the god. Dignity and splendor are not properties beside and behind which the god, too, stands as something distinct, but it is rather in the dignity, in the splendor that the god is present. In the reflected glory of this splendor there glows, i.e., there lightens itself, what we called the word. To e-rect means: to open the right in the sense of a guiding measure, a form in which what belongs to the nature of being gives guidance. But why is the setting up of a work an erecting that consecrates and praises? Because the work, in its work-being, demands it. How is it that the work comes to demand such a setting up? Because it itself, in its own work-being, is something that sets up. What does the work, as work, set up? Towering up within itself, the work opens up a *world* and keeps it abidingly in force.

To be a work means to set up a world. But what is it to be a world? The answer was hinted at when we referred to the temple. On the path we must follow here, the nature of world can only be indicated. What is more, this indication limits itself to warding off anything that might at first distort our view of the world's nature.

The world is not the mere collection of the countable or uncountable, familiar and unfamiliar things that are just there. But neither is it a merely imagined framework added by our representation to the sum of such given things. The *world worlds,* and is more fully in being than the tangible and perceptible realm in which we believe ourselves to be at home. World is never an object that stands before us and can be seen. World is the ever-nonobjective to which we are subject as long as the paths of birth and death, blessing and curse keep us transported into Being. Wherever those decisions of our history that relate to our very being are made, are taken up and abandoned by us, go unrecognized and are rediscovered by new inquiry, there the world worlds. A stone is worldless. Plant and animal likewise have no world; but they belong to the covert throng of a surrounding into which they are linked. The peasant woman, on the other hand, has a world because she dwells in the overtness of beings, of the things that are. Her equipment, in its reliability, gives to this world a necessity and nearness of its own. By the opening up of a world, all things gain their lingering and hastening, their remoteness and nearness, their scope and limits. In a world's worlding is gathered that spaciousness out of which the protective grace of the gods is granted or withheld. Even this doom of the god remaining absent is a way in which world worlds.

A work, by being a work, makes space for that spaciousness. "To make space for" means here especially to liberate the Open and to establish it in its structure. This in-stalling occurs through the erecting mentioned earlier. The work as work sets up a world. The work holds open the Open of the world. But the setting up of a world is only the first essential feature in the work-being of a work to be referred to here. Starting again from the foreground of the work, we shall attempt to make clear in the same way the second essential feature that belongs with the first.

When a work is created, brought forth out of this or that work-material—stone, wood, metal, color, language, tone—we say also that it is made, set forth out of it. But just as the work requires a setting up in the sense of a consecrating-praising erection, because the work's work-being consists in the setting up of a world, so a setting forth is needed because the work-being of the work itself has the character of setting forth. The work as work, in its presencing, is a setting forth, a making. But what does the work set forth? We come to know about this only when we explore what comes to the fore and is customarily spoken of as the making or production of works.

To work-being there belongs the setting up of a world.

Thinking of it within this perspective, what is the nature of that in the work which is usually called the work material? Because it is determined by usefulness and serviceability, equipment takes into its service that of which it consists: the matter. In fabricating equipment—e.g., an ax—stone is used, and used up. It disappears into usefulness. The material is all the better and more suitable the less it resists perishing in the equipmental being of the equipment. By contrast the temple-work, in setting up a world, does not cause the material to disappear, but rather causes it to come forth for the very first time and to come into the Open of the work's world. The rock comes to bear and rest and so first becomes rock; metals come to glitter and shimmer, colors to glow, tones to sing, the word to speak. All this comes forth as the work sets itself back into the massiveness and heaviness of stone, into the firmness and pliancy of wood, into the hardness and luster of metal, into the lighting and darkening of color, into the clang of tone, and into the naming power of the word.

That into which the work sets itself back and which it causes to come forth in this setting back of itself we called the earth. Earth is that which comes forth and shelters. Earth, self-dependent, is effortless and untiring. Upon the earth and in it, historical man grounds his dwelling in the world. In setting up a world, the work sets forth the earth. This setting forth must be thought here in the strict sense of the word. The work moves the earth itself into the Open of a world and keeps it there. *The work lets the earth be an earth.*

But why must this setting forth of the earth happen in such a way that the work sets itself back into it? What is the earth that it attains to the unconcealed in just such a manner? A stone presses downward and manifests its heaviness. But while this heaviness exerts an opposing pressure upon us it denies us any penetration into it. If we attempt such a penetration by breaking open the rock, it still does not display in its fragments anything inward that has been disclosed. The stone has instantly withdrawn again into the same dull pressure and bulk of its fragments. If we try to lay hold of the stone's heaviness in another way, by placing the stone on a balance, we merely bring the heaviness into the form of a calculated weight. This perhaps very precise determination of the stone remains a number, but the weight's burden has escaped us. Color shines and wants only to shine. When we analyze it in rational terms by measuring its wavelengths, it is gone. It shows itself only when it remains undisclosed and unexplained. Earth thus shatters every attempt to penetrate into it. It causes every merely calculating importunity upon it to turn into a destruction. This destruction may herald itself under the appearance of mastery and of progress in the form of the technical-scientific objectivation of nature, but this mastery nevertheless remains an impotence of will. The earth appears openly cleared as itself only when it is perceived and preserved as that which is by nature undisclosable, that which shrinks from every disclosure and constantly keeps itself closed up. All things of earth, and the earth itself as a whole, flow together into a reciprocal accord. But this confluence is not a blurring of their outlines. Here there flows the stream, restful within itself, of the setting of bounds, which delimits everything present within its presence. Thus in each of the self-secluding things there is the same not-knowing-of-one-another. The earth is essentially self-secluding. To set forth the earth means to bring it into the Open as the self-secluding.

This setting forth of the earth is achieved by the work as it sets itself back into the earth. The self-seclusion of earth, however, is not a uniform, inflexible staying under cover, but unfolds itself in an inexhaustible variety of simple modes and shapes. To be sure, the sculptor uses stone just as the mason uses it, in his own way. But he does not use it up. That happens in a certain way only where the work miscarries. To be sure, the painter also uses pigment, but in such a way that color is not used up but rather only now comes to shine forth. To be sure, the poet also uses the word—not, however, like ordinary speakers and writers who have to use them up, but rather in such a way that the word only now becomes and remains truly a word.

Nowhere in the work is there any trace of a work-material. It even remains doubtful whether, in the essential definition of equipment, what the equipment consists of is properly described in its equipmental nature as matter.

The setting up of a world and the setting forth of earth are two essential features in the work-being of the work. They belong together, however, in the unity of work-being. This is the unity we seek when we ponder the self-subsistence of the work and try to express in words this closed, unitary repose of self-support.

But in the essential features just mentioned, if our account has any validity at all, we have indicated in the work rather a happening and in no sense a repose, for what is rest if not the opposite of motion? It is at any rate not an opposite that excludes motion from itself, but rather includes it. Only what is in motion can rest. The mode of rest varies with the kind of motion. In motion as the mere displacement of a body, rest is, to be sure, only the limiting case of motion. Where rest includes motion, there can exist a repose which is an inner concentration of motion, hence a highest state of agitation, assuming that the mode of motion requires such a rest. Now the repose of the work that rests in itself is of this sort. We shall therefore come nearer to this repose if we can succeed in grasping the state of movement of the happening in work-being in its full unity. We ask: What relation do the setting up of a world and the setting forth of the earth exhibit in the work itself?

The world is the self-disclosing openness of the broad paths of the simple and essential decisions in the destiny of an historical people. The earth is the spontaneous forthcoming of that which is continually self-secluding and to that extent sheltering and concealing. World and earth are essentially different from one another and yet are never separated. The world grounds itself on the earth, and earth juts through world. But the relation between world and earth does not wither away into the empty unity of opposites unconcerned with one another. The world, in resting upon the earth, strives to surmount it. As self-opening it cannot endure anything closed. The earth, however, as sheltering and concealing, tends always to draw the world into itself and keep it there.

The opposition of world and earth is a striving. But we would surely all too easily falsify its nature if we were to confound striving with discord and dispute, and thus see it only as disorder and destruction. In essential striving, rather, the opponents raise each other into the self-assertion of their natures. Self-assertion of nature, however, is never a rigid insistence upon some contingent state, but surrender to the concealed originality of the source of one's own being. In the struggle, each opponent carries the other beyond itself. Thus the striving becomes ever more intense as striving, and more authentically what it is. The more the struggle overdoes itself on its own part, the more inflexibly do the opponents let themselves go into the intimacy of simple belonging to one another. The earth cannot dispense with the Open of the world if it itself is to appear as earth in the liberated surge of its self-seclusion. The world, again, cannot soar out of the earth's sight if, as the governing breadth and path of all essential destiny, it is to ground itself on a resolute foundation.

In setting up a world and setting forth the earth, the work is an instigating of this striving. This does not happen so that the work should at the same time settle and put an end to the conflict in an insipid agreement, but so that the strife may remain a strife. Setting up a world and setting forth the earth, the work accomplishes this striving. The work-being of the work consists in the fighting of the battle between world and earth. It is because the struggle arrives at its high point in the simplicity of intimacy that the unity of the work comes about in the fighting of the battle. The fighting of the battle is the continually self-overreaching gathering of the work's agitation. The repose of the work that rests in itself thus has its presencing in the intimacy of striving.

From this repose of the work we can now first see what is at work in the work. Until now it was a merely provisional assertion that in an art work the truth is set to work. In what way does truth happen in the work-being of the work, i.e., now, how does truth happen in the fighting of the battle between world and earth? What is truth?

How slight and stunted our knowledge of the nature of truth is, is shown by the laxity we permit ourselves in using this basic word. By truth is usually meant this or that particular truth. That means: something true. A cognition articulated in a proposition can be of this sort. However, we call not only a proposition true, but also a thing, true gold in contrast with sham gold. True here means genuine, real gold. What does the expression "real" mean here? To us it is what is in truth. The true is what corresponds to the real, and the real is what is in truth. The circle has closed again.

What does "in truth" mean? Truth is the essence of the true. What do we have in mind when speaking of essence? Usually it is thought to be those features held in common by everything that is true. The essence is discovered in the generic and universal concept, which represents the one feature that holds indifferently for many things. This indifferent essence (essentiality in the sense of *essentia*) is, however, only the inessential essence. What does the essential essence of something consist in? Presumably it lies in what the entity *is* in truth. The true essential nature of a thing is determined by way of its true being, by way of the truth of the given being. But we are now seeking not the truth of essential nature but the essential nature of truth. There thus appears a curious tangle. Is it only a curiosity or even merely the empty sophistry of a conceptual game, or is it—an abyss?

Truth means the nature of the true. We think this nature in recollecting the Greek word *aletheia,* the unconcealedness of beings. But is this enough to define the nature of truth? Are we not passing off a mere change of word usage—unconcealedness instead of truth—as a characterization of fact? Certainly we do not get beyond an interchange of names as long as we do not come to know what must have happened in order to be compelled to tell the *nature* of truth in the word "unconcealed-ness."

Does this require a revival of Greek philosophy? Not at all. A revival, even if such an impossibility were possible, would be of no help to us; for the hidden history of Greek philosophy consists from its beginning in this, that it does not remain in conformity with the nature of truth that flashes out in the word *aletheia,* and has to misdirect its knowing and its speaking about the nature of truth more and more into the discussion of a derivative nature of truth. The nature of truth as *aletheia* was not thought out in the thinking of the Greeks nor since then, and least of all in the philosophy that followed after. Uncon-cealedness is, for thought, the most concealed thing in Greek existence, although from early times it determines the presence of everything present.

Yet why should we not be satisfied with the nature of truth that has by now been familiar to us for centuries? Truth means today and has long meant the agreement or conformity of knowledge with fact. However, the fact must show itself to be fact if knowledge and the proposition that forms and expresses knowledge are to be able to conform to the fact; otherwise the fact cannot become binding on the proposition. How can fact show itself if it cannot itself stand forth out of concealedness, if it does not itself stand in the unconcealed? A proposition is true by conforming to the unconcealed, to what is true. Propo-sitional truth is always, and always exclusively, this correctness. The critical concepts of truth which, since Descartes, start out from truth as certainty, are merely variations of the definition of truth as correctness. This nature of truth which is familiar to us—correctness in representation—stands and falls with truth as unconcealedness of beings.

If here and elsewhere we conceive of truth as unconcealedness, we are not merely taking refuge in a more literal translation of a Greek word. We are reminding ourselves of what, unexperienced and unthought, underlies our familiar and therefore outworn nature of truth in the sense of correctness. We do, of course, occasionally take the trouble to concede that naturally, in order to understand and verify the correctness (truth) of a proposition one really should go back to something that is already evident, and that this presupposition is indeed unavoidable. As long as we talk and believe in this way, we always understand truth merely as correctness, which of course still requires a further presupposition, that we ourselves just happen to make, heaven knows how or why.

But it is not we who presuppose the unconcealedness of beings; rather, the unconcealedness of beings (Being) puts us into such a condition of being that in our representation we always remain installed within and in attendance upon unconcealedness. Not only must that in *conformity* with which a cognition orders itself be already in some way unconcealed. The entire *realm* in which this "conforming to something" goes on must already occur as a whole in the unconcealed; and this holds equally of that *for* which the conformity of a proposition to fact becomes manifest. With all our correct representations we would get nowhere, we could not even presuppose that there already is manifest something to which we can conform ourselves, unless the unconcealedness of beings had already exposed us to, placed us in that lighted realm in which every being stands for us and from which it withdraws.

But how does this take place? How does truth happen as this unconcealedness? First, however, we must say more clearly what this unconcealedness itself is.

Things are, and human beings, gifts, and sacrifices are, animals and plants are, equipment and works are. That which is, the particular being, stands in Being. Through Being there passes a veiled destiny that is ordained between the godly and the countergodly. There is much in being that man cannot master. There is but little that comes to be known. What is known remains inexact, what is mastered insecure. What is, is never of our making or even merely the product of our minds, as it might all too easily seem. When we contemplate this whole as one, then we apprehend, so it appears, all that is— though we grasp it crudely enough.

And yet—beyond what is, not away from it but before it, there is still something else that happens. In the midst of beings as a whole an open place occurs. There is a clearing, a lighting. Thought of in reference to what is, to beings, this clearing is in a greater degree than are beings. This open center is therefore not surrounded by what is; rather, the lighting center itself encircles all that is, like the Nothing which we scarcely know.

That which is can only be, as a being, if it stands within and stands out within what is lighted in this clearing. Only this clearing grants and guarantees to us humans a passage to those beings that we ourselves are not, and access to the being that we ourselves are. Thanks to this clearing, beings are uncon-cealed in certain changing degrees. And yet a being can be *concealed,* too, only within the sphere of what is lighted. Each being we encounter and which encounters us keeps to this curious opposition of presence in that it always withholds itself at the same time in a concealedness. The clearing in which be-ings stand is in itself at the same time concealment. Conceal-ment, however, prevails in the midst of beings in a twofold way.

Beings refuse themselves to us down to that one and seem-ingly least feature which we touch upon most readily when we can say no more of beings than that they are. Concealment as refusal is not simply and only the limit of knowledge in any given circumstance, but the beginning of the clearing of what is lighted. But concealment, though of another sort, to be sure, at the same time also occurs within what is lighted. One being places itself in front of another being, the one helps to hide the other, the former obscures the latter, a few obstruct many, one denies all. Here concealment is not simple refusal. Rather, a being appears, but it presents itself as other than it is.

This concealment is dissembling. If one being did not simulate another, we could not make mistakes or act mistakenly in regard to beings; we could not go astray and transgress, and especially could never overreach ourselves. That a being should be able to deceive as semblance is the condition for our being able to be deceived, not conversely.

Concealment can be a refusal or merely a dissembling. We are never fully certain whether it is the one or the other. Concealment conceals and dissembles itself. This means: the open place in the midst of beings, the clearing, is never a rigid stage with a permanently raised curtain on which the play of beings runs its course. Rather, the clearing happens only as this double concealment. The unconcealedness of beings—this is never a merely existent state, but a happening. Unconcealedness (truth) is neither an attribute of factual things in the sense of beings, nor one of propositions.

We believe we are at home in the immediate circle of beings. That which is, is familiar, reliable, ordinary. Nevertheless, the clearing is pervaded by a constant concealment in the double form of refusal and dissembling. At bottom, the ordinary is not ordinary; it is extra-ordinary, uncanny. The nature of truth, that is, of unconcealedness, is dominated throughout by a denial. Yet this denial is not a defect or a fault, as though truth were an unalloyed unconcealedness that has rid itself of everything concealed. If truth could accomplish this, it would no longer be itself. *This denial, in the form of a double concealment, belongs to the nature of truth as unconcealedness.* Truth, in its nature, is un-truth. We put the matter this way in order to serve notice, with a possibly surprising trenchancy, that denial in the manner of concealment belongs to unconcealedness as clearing. The proposition, "the nature of truth is untruth," is not, however, intended to state that truth is at bottom falsehood. Nor does it mean that truth is never itself but, viewed dialectically, is always also its opposite.

Truth occurs precisely as itself in that the concealing denial, as refusal, provides its constant source to all clearing, and yet, as dissembling, it metes out to all clearing the indefeasible severity of error. Concealing denial is intended to denote that opposition in the nature of truth which subsists between clearing, or lighting, and concealing. It is the opposition of the primal conflict. The nature of truth is, in itself, the primal conflict in which that open center is won within which what is, stands, and from which it sets itself back into itself.

This Open happens in the midst of beings. It exhibits an essential feature which we have already mentioned. To the Open there belong a world and the earth. But the world is not simply the Open that corresponds to clearing, and the earth is not simply the Closed that corresponds to concealment. Rather, the world is the clearing of the paths of the essential guiding directions with which all decision complies. Every decision, however, bases itself on something not mastered, something concealed, confusing; else it would never be a decision. The earth is not simply the Closed but rather that which rises up as self-closing. World and earth are always intrinsically and essentially in conflict, belligerent by nature. Only as such do they enter into the conflict of clearing and concealing.

Earth juts through the world and world grounds itself on the earth only so far as truth happens as the primal conflict between clearing and concealing. But how does truth happen? We answer: it happens in a few essential ways. One of these ways in which truth happens is the work-being of the work. Setting up a world and setting forth the earth, the work is the fighting of the battle in which the unconcealedness of beings as a whole, or truth, is won.

Truth happens in the temple's standing where it is. This does not mean that something is correctly represented and rendered here, but that what is as a whole is brought into unconcealedness and held therein. To hold (*halten*) originally means to tend, keep, take care (*hüten*). Truth happens in Van Gogh's painting. This does not mean that something is correctly portrayed, but rather that in the revelation of the equipmental being of the shoes, that which is as a whole—world and earth in their counterplay—attains to unconcealedness.

Thus in the work it is truth, not only something true, that is at work. The picture that shows the peasant shoes, the poem that says the Roman fountain, do not just make manifest what this isolated being as such is—if indeed they manifest anything at all; rather, they make unconcealedness as such happen in regard to what is as a whole. The more simply and authentically the shoes are engrossed in their nature, the more plainly and purely the fountain is engrossed in its nature—the more directly and engagingly do all beings attain to a greater degree of being along with them. That is how self-concealing being is illuminated. Light of this kind joins its shining to and into the work. This shining, joined in the work, is the beautiful. *Beauty is one way in which truth occurs as unconcealedness.*

We now, indeed, grasp the nature of truth more clearly in certain respects. What is at work in the work may accordingly have become more clear. But the work's now visible work-being still does not tell us anything about the work's closest and most obtrusive reality, about the thingly aspect of the work. Indeed it almost seems as though, in pursuing the exclusive aim of grasping the work's independence as purely as possible, we had completely overlooked the one thing, that a work is always a work, which means that it is something worked out, brought about, effected. If there is anything that distinguishes the work as work, it is that the work has been created. Since the work is created, and creation requires a medium out of which and in which it creates, the thingly element, too, enters into the work.

This is incontestable. Still the question remains: how does being created belong to the work? This can be elucidated only if two points are cleared up:

1. What do being created and creation mean here in distinction from making and being made?

2. What is the inmost nature of the work itself, from which alone can be gauged how far createdness belongs to the work and how far it determines the work-being of the work?

Creation is here always thought of in reference to the work. To the nature of the work there belongs the happening of truth. From the outset we define the nature of creating by its relation to the nature of truth as the unconcealedness of beings. The pertinence of createdness to the work can be elucidated only by way of a more fundamental clarification of the nature of truth. The question of truth and its nature returns again.

We must raise that question once more, if the proposition that truth is at work in the work is not to remain a mere assertion.

We must now first ask in a more essential way: how does the impulse toward such a thing as a work lie in the nature of truth? Of what nature is truth, that it can be set into work, or even under certain conditions must be set into work, in order to be *as* truth? But we defined the setting-into-a-work of truth as the nature of art. Hence our last question becomes:

What is truth, that it can happen as, or even must happen as, art? How is it that art exists at all?

Truth and Art

Art is the origin of the art work and of the artist. Origin is the source of the nature in which the being of an entity is present. What is art? We seek its nature in the actual work. The actual reality of the work has been defined by that which is at work in the work, by the happening of truth. This happening we think of as the fighting of the conflict between world and earth. Repose occurs in the concentrated agitation of this conflict. The independence or self-composure of the work is grounded here.

In the work, the happening of truth is at work. But what is thus at work, is so *in* the work. This means that the actual work is here already presupposed as the bearer of this happening. At once the problem of the thingly feature of the given work confronts us again. One thing thus finally becomes clear: however zealously we inquire into the work's self-sufficiency, we shall still fail to find its actuality as long as we do not also agree to take the work as something worked, effected. To take it thus lies closest at hand, for in the word "work" we hear what is worked. The workly character of the work consists in its having been created by the artist. It may seem curious that this most obvious and all-clarifying definition of the work is mentioned only now.

The work's createdness, however, can obviously be grasped only in terms of the process of creation. Thus, constrained by the facts, we must consent after all to go into the activity of the artist in order to arrive at the origin of the work of art. The attempt to define the work-being of the work purely in terms of the work itself proves to be unfeasible.

In turning away now from the work to examine the nature of the creative process, we should like nevertheless to keep in mind what was said first of the picture of the peasant shoes and later of the Greek temple.

We think of creation as a bringing forth. But the making of equipment, too, is a bringing forth. Handicraft—a remarkable play of language—does not, to be sure, create works, not even when we contrast, as we must, the handmade with the factory product. But what is it that distinguishes bringing forth as creation from bringing forth in the mode of making? It is as difficult to track down the essential features of the creation of works and the making of equipment as it is easy to distinguish verbally between the two modes of bringing forth. Going along with first appearances we find the same procedure in the activity of potter and sculptor, of joiner and painter. The creation of a work requires craftsmanship. Great artists prize craftmanship most highly. They are the first to call for its painstaking cultivation, based on complete mastery. They above all others constantly strive to educate themselves ever anew in thorough craftsmanship. It has often enough been pointed out that the Greeks, who knew quite a bit about works of art, use the same word *techne* for craft and art and call the craftsman and the artist by the same name: *technites*.

It thus seems advisable to define the nature of creative work in terms of its craft aspect. But reference to the linguistic usage of the Greeks, with their experience of the facts, must give us pause. However usual and convincing the reference may be to the Greek practice of naming craft and art by the same name, *techne,* it nevertheless remains oblique and superficial; for *techne* signifies neither craft nor art, and not at all the technical in our present-day sense; it never means a kind of practical performance.

The word *techne* denotes rather a mode of knowing. To know means to have seen, in the widest sense of seeing, which means to apprehend what is present, as such. For Greek thought the nature of knowing consists in *aletheia,* that is, in the uncovering of beings. It supports and guides all comportment toward beings. *Techne,* as knowledge experienced in the Greek manner, is a bringing forth of beings in that it *brings forth* present beings as such beings *out of* concealedness and specifically *into* the unconcealedness of their appearance; *techne* never signifies the action of making.

The artist is a *technites* not because he is also a craftsman, but because both the setting forth of works and the setting forth of equipment occur in a bringing forth and presenting that causes beings in the first place to come forward and be present in assuming an appearance. Yet all this happens in the midst of the being that grows out of its own accord, *phusis.* Calling art *techne* does not at all imply that the artist's action is seen in the light of craft. What looks like craft in the creation of a work is of a different sort. This doing is determined and pervaded by the nature of creation, and indeed remains contained within that creating.

What then, if not craft, is to guide our thinking about the nature of creation? What else than a view of what is to be created: the work? Although it becomes actual only as the creative act is performed, and thus depends for its reality upon this act, the nature of creation is determined by the nature of the work. Even though the work's createdness has a relation to creation, nevertheless both createdness and creation must be defined in terms of the work-being of the work. And now it can no longer seem strange that we first and at length dealt with the work alone, to bring its createdness into view only at the end. If createdness belongs to the work as essentially as the word "work" makes it sound, then we must try to understand even more essentially what so far could be defined as the work-being of the work.

In the light of the definition of the work we have reached at this point, according to which the happening of truth is at work in the work, we are able to characterize creation as follows: to create is to cause something to emerge as a thing that has been brought forth. The work's becoming a work is a way in which truth becomes and happens. It all rests on the nature of truth. But what is truth, that it has to happen in such a thing as something created? How does truth have an impulse toward a work grounded in its very nature? Is this intelligible in terms of the nature of truth as thus far elucidated?

Truth is un-truth, insofar as there belongs to it the reservoir of the not-yet-uncovered, the un-uncovered, in the sense of concealment. In unconcealedness, as truth, there occurs also the other "un-" of a double restraint or refusal. Truth occurs as such in the opposition of clearing and double concealing. Truth is the primal conflict in which, always in some particular way, the Open is won within which everything stands and from which everything withholds itself that shows itself and withdraws itself as a being. Whenever and however this conflict breaks out and happens, the opponents, lighting or clearing and concealing, move apart because of it. Thus the Open of the place of conflict is won. The openness of this Open, that is, truth, can be what it is, namely, *this* openness, only if and as long as it establishes itself within its Open. Hence there must always be some being in this Open, something that is, in which the openness takes its stand and attains its constancy. In taking possession thus of the Open, the openness holds open the Open and sustains it. Setting and taking possession are here everywhere drawn from the Greek sense of *thesis,* which means a setting up in the unconcealed.

In referring to this self-establishing of openness in the Open, thinking touches on a sphere that cannot yet be explicated here. Only this much should be noted, that if the nature of the unconcealedness of beings belongs in any way to Being itself (cf. *Being and Time,* § 44*), then Being, by way of its own nature, lets the place of openness (the lighting-clearing of the There) happen, and introduces it as a place of the sort in which each being emerges or arises in its own way.

Truth happens only by establishing itself in the conflict and sphere opened up by truth itself. Because truth is the opposition of clearing and concealing, there belongs to it what is here to be called establishing. But truth does not exist in itself beforehand, somewhere among the stars, only later to descend elsewhere among beings. This is impossible for the reason alone that it is after all only the openness of beings that first affords the possibility of a somewhere and of a place filled by present beings. Clearing of openness and establishment in the Open belong together. They are the same single nature of the happening of truth. This happening is historical in many ways.

One essential way in which truth establishes itself in the

---

* Martin Heidegger, *Being and Time,* translated by John Macquarrie and Edward Robinson, New York: Harper & Row, 1962.—Tr.

beings it has opened up is truth setting itself into work. Another way in which truth occurs is the act that founds a political state. Still another way in which truth comes to shine forth is the nearness of that which is not simply a being, but the being that is most of all. Still another way in which truth grounds itself is the essential sacrifice. Still another way in which truth becomes is the thinker's questioning, which, as the thinking of Being, names Being in its question-worthiness. By contrast, science is not an original happening of truth, but always the cultivation of a domain of truth already opened, specifically by apprehending and confirming that which shows itself to be possibly and necessarily correct within that field. When and insofar as a science passes beyond correctness and goes on to a truth, which means that it arrives at the essential disclosure of what is as such, it is philosophy.

Because it is in the nature of truth to establish itself within that which is, in order thus first to become truth, therefore the impulse toward the work lies in the nature of truth as one of truth's distinctive possibilities by which it can itself occur as being in the midst of beings.

The establishing of truth in the work is the bringing forth of a being such as never was before and will never come to be again. The bringing forth places this being in the Open in such a way that what is to be brought forth first clears the openness of the Open into which it comes forth. Where this bringing forth expressly brings the openness of beings, or truth, that which is brought forth is a work. Creation is such a bringing forth. As such a bringing, it is rather a receiving and an incorporating of a relation to unconcealedness. What, accordingly, does the createdness consist in? It may be elucidated by two essential determinations.

Truth establishes itself in the work. Truth is present only as the conflict between lighting and concealing in the opposition of world and earth. Truth wills to be established in the work as this conflict of world and earth. The conflict is not to be resolved in a being brought forth for the purpose, nor is it to be merely housed there; the conflict, on the contrary, is started by it. This being must therefore contain within itself the essential traits of the conflict. In the strife the unity of world and earth is won. As a world opens itself, it submits to the decision of an historical humanity the question of victory and defeat, blessing and curse, mastery and slavery. The dawning world brings out what is as yet undecided and measureless, and thus discloses the hidden necessity of measure and decisiveness.

But as a world opens itself the earth comes to rise up. It stands forth as that which bears all, as that which is sheltered in its own law and always wrapped up in itself. World demands its decisiveness and its measure and lets beings attain to the Open of their paths. Earth, bearing and jutting, strives to keep itself closed and to entrust everything to its law. The conflict is not a rift (*Riss*) as a mere cleft is ripped open; rather, it is the intimacy with which opponents belong to each other. This rift carries the opponents into the source of their unity by virtue of their common ground. It is a basic design, an outline sketch, that draws the basic features of the rise of the lighting of beings. This rift does not let the opponents break apart; it brings the opposition of measure and boundary into their common outline.

Truth establishes itself as a strife within a being that is to be brought forth only in such a way that the conflict opens up in this being, that is, this being is itself brought into the rift-design. The rift-design is the drawing together, into a unity, of sketch and basic design, breach and outline. Truth establishes itself in a being in such a way, indeed, that this being itself occupies the Open of truth. This occupying, however, can happen only if what is to be brought forth, the rift, entrusts itself to the self-secluding factor that juts up in the Open. The rift must set itself back into the heavy weight of stone, the dumb hardness of wood, the dark glow of colors. As the earth takes the rift back into itself, the rift is first set forth into the Open and thus placed, that is, set, within that which towers up into the Open as self-closing and sheltering.

The strife that is brought into the rift and thus set back into the earth and thus fixed in place is *figure, shape, Gestalt*. Createdness of the work means: truth's being fixed in place in the figure. Figure is the structure in whose shape the rift composes and submits itself. This composed rift is the fitting or joining of the shining of truth. What is here called figure, *Gestalt*, is always to be thought in terms of the particular placing (*Stellen*) and framing or framework (*Ge-stell*) as which the work occurs when it sets itself up and sets itself forth.

In the creation of a work, the conflict, as rift, must be set back into the earth, and the earth itself must be set forth and used as the self-closing factor. This use, however, does not use up or misuse the earth as matter, but rather sets it free to be nothing but itself. This use of the earth is a working with it that, to be sure, looks like the employment of matter in handicraft. Hence the appearance that artistic creation is also an activity of handicraft. It never is. But it is at all times a use of the earth in the fixing in place of truth in the figure. In contrast, the making of equipment is never directly the effecting of the happening of truth. The production of equipment is finished when a material has been so formed as to be ready for use. For equipment to be ready means that it is dismissed beyond itself, to be used up in serviceability.

Not so when a work is created. This becomes clear in the light of the second characteristic, which may be introduced here.

The readiness of equipment and the createdness of the work agree in this, that in each case something is produced. But in contrast to all other modes of production, the work is distinguished by being created so that its createdness is part of the created work. But does not this hold true for everything brought forth, indeed for anything that has in any way come to be? Everything brought forth surely has this endowment of having been brought forth, if it has any endowment at all. Certainly.

But in the work, createdness is expressly created into the created being, so that it stands out from it, from the being thus brought forth, in an expressly particular way. If this is how matters stand, then we must also be able to discover and experience the createdness explicitly in the work.

The emergence of createdness from the work does not mean that the work is to give the impression of having been made by a great artist. The point is not that the created being be certified as the performance of a capable person, so that the producer is thereby brought to public notice. It is not the "N. N. fecit" that is to be made known. Rather, the simple "factum est" is to be held forth into the Open by the work: namely this, that unconcealedness of what is has happened here, and that as this happening it happens here for the first time; or, that such a work *is* at all rather than is not. The thrust that the work as this work is, and the uninterruptedness of this plain thrust, constitute the steadfastness of the work's self-subsistence. Precisely where the artist and the process and the circumstances of the genesis of the work remain unknown, this thrust, this *"that* it is" of createdness, emerges into view most purely from the work.

To be sure, "that" it is made is a property also of all equipment that is available and in use. But this "that" does not become prominent in the equipment; it disappears in usefulness. The more handy a piece of equipment is, the more inconspicuous it remains that, for example, such a hammer is and the more exclusively does the equipment keep itself in its equipmentality. In general, of everything present to us, we can note that it *is;* but this also, if it is noted at all, is noted only soon to fall into oblivion, as is the wont of everything commonplace. And what is more commonplace than this, that a being is? In a work, by contrast, this fact, that it *is* as a work, is just what is unusual. The event of its being created does not simply reverberate through the work; rather, the work casts before itself the eventful fact that the work is as this work, and it has constantly this fact about itself. The more essentially the work opens itself, the more luminous becomes the uniqueness of the fact that it is rather than is not. The more essentially this thrust comes into the Open, the stronger and more solitary the work becomes. In the bringing forth of the work there lies this offering "that it be."

The question of the work's createdness ought to have brought us nearer to its workly character and therewith to its reality. Createdness revealed itself as the conflict's being fixed in place in the figure by means of the rift. Createdness here is itself expressly created into the work and stands as the silent thrust into the Open of the "that." But the work's reality does not exhaust itself even in createdness. However, this view of the nature of the work's createdness now enables us to take the step toward which everything thus far said tends.

The more solitarily the work, fixed in the figure, stands on its own and the more cleanly it seems to cut all ties to human beings, the more simply does the thrust come into the Open that such a work *is,* and the more essentially is the extraordinary thrust to the surface and the long-familiar thrust down. But this multiple thrusting is nothing violent, for the more purely the work is itself transported into the openness of beings—an openness opened by itself—the more simply does it transport us into this openness and thus at the same time transport us out of the realm of the ordinary. To submit to this displacement means: to transform our accustomed ties to world and to earth and henceforth to restrain all usual doing and prizing, knowing and looking, in order to stay within the truth that is happening in the work. Only the restraint of this staying lets what is created be the work that it is. This letting the work be a work we call the preserving of the work. It is only for such preserving that the work yields itself in its createdness as actual, i.e., now: present in the manner of a work.

Just as a work cannot be without being created but is essentially in need of creators, so what is created cannot itself come into being without those who preserve it.

However, if a work does not find preservers, does not at once find them such as respond to the truth happening in the work, this does not at all mean that the work may also be a work without preservers. Being a work, it always remains tied to preservers, even and particularly when it is still only waiting for preservers and only pleads and waits for them to enter into its truth. Even the oblivion into which the work can sink is not nothing; it is still a preservation. It feeds on the work. Preserving the work means: standing within the openness of beings that happens in the work. This "standing-within" of preservation, however, is a knowing. Yet knowing does not consist in mere information and notions about something. He who truly knows what is, knows what he wills to do in the midst of what is.

The willing here referred to, which neither merely applies knowledge nor decides beforehand, is thought of in terms of the basic experience of thinking in *Being and Time*. Knowing that remains a willing, and willing that remains a knowing, is the existing human being's entrance into and compliance with the unconcealedness of Being. The resoluteness intended in *Being and Time* is not the deliberate action of a subject, but the opening up of human being, out of its captivity in that which is, to the openness of Being.* However, in existence, man does not proceed from some inside to some outside; rather, the nature of *Existenz* is out-standing standing-within the essential sunderance of the clearing of beings. Neither in the creation mentioned before nor in the willing mentioned now do we think of the performance or act of a subject striving toward himself as his self-set goal.

Willing is the sober resolution of that existential self-transcendence which exposes itself to the openness of beings as it is set into the work. In this way, standing-within is brought under law. Preserving the work, as knowing, is a sober standing-

---

* The word for resoluteness, *Entschlossenheit,* if taken literally, would mean "unclosedness."—Tr.

within the extraordinary awesomeness of the truth that is happening in the work.

This knowledge, which as a willing makes its home in the work's truth and only thus remains a knowing, does not deprive the work of its independence, does not drag it into the sphere of mere experience, and does not degrade it to the role of a stimulator of experience. Preserving the work does not reduce people to their private experiences, but brings them into affiliation with the truth happening in the work. Thus it grounds being for and with one another as the historical standing-out of human existence in reference to unconcealedness. Most of all, knowledge in the manner of preserving is far removed from that merely aestheticizing connoisseurship of the work's formal aspects, its qualities and charms. Knowing as having seen is a being resolved; it is standing within the conflict that the work has fitted into the rift.

The proper way to preserve the work is cocreated and prescribed only and exclusively by the work. Preserving occurs at different levels of knowledge, with always differing degrees of scope, constancy, and lucidity. When works are offered for merely artistic enjoyment, this does not yet prove that they stand in preservation as works.

As soon as the thrust into the extraordinary is parried and captured by the sphere of familiarity and connoisseurship, the art business has begun. Even a painstaking handing on of works to posterity, all scientific efforts to regain them, no longer reach the work's own being, but only a recollection of it. But even this recollection may still offer to the work a place from which it joins in shaping history. The work's own peculiar reality, on the other hand, is brought to bear only where the work is preserved in the truth that happens by the work itself.

The work's reality is determined in its basic features by the nature of the work's being. We can now return to our opening question: how do matters stand with the work's thingly feature that is to guarantee its immediate reality? They stand so that now we no longer raise this question about the work's thingly element; for as long as we ask it, we take the work directly and as a foregone conclusion, as an object that is simply there. In that way we never question in terms of the work, but in our own terms. In our terms—we, who then do not let the work be a work but view it as an object that is supposed to produce this or that state of mind in us.

But what looks like the thingly element, in the sense of our usual thing-concepts, in the work taken as object, is, seen from the perspective of the work, its earthy character. The earth juts up within the work because the work exists as something in which truth is at work and because truth occurs only by installing itself within a particular being. In the earth, however, as essentially self-closing, the openness of the Open finds the greatest resistance (to the Open) and thereby the site of the Open's constant stand, where the figure must be fixed in place.

Was it then superfluous, after all, to enter into the question of the thingly character of the thing? By no means. To be sure, the work's work-character cannot be defined in terms of its thingly character, but as against that the question about the thing's thingly character can be brought into the right course by way of a knowledge of the work's work-character. This is no small matter, if we recollect that those ancient, traditional modes of thought attack the thing's thingly character and make it subject to an interpretation of what is as a whole, which remains unfit to apprehend the nature of equipment and of the work, and which makes us equally blind to the original nature of truth.

To determine the thing's thingness neither consideration of the bearer of properties is adequate, nor that of the manifold of sense data in their unity, and least of all that of the matter-form structure regarded by itself, which is derived from equipment. Anticipating a meaningful and weighty interpretation of the thingly character of things, we must aim at the thing's belonging to the earth. The nature of the earth, in its free and unhurried bearing and self-closure, reveals itself, however, only in the earth's jutting into a world, in the opposition of the two. This conflict is fixed in place in the figure of the work and becomes manifest by it. What holds true of equipment—namely that we come to know its equipmental character specifically only through the work itself—also holds of the thingly character of the thing. The fact that we never know thingness directly, and if we know it at all, then only vaguely and thus require the work—this fact proves indirectly that in the work's work-being the happening of truth, the opening up or disclosure of what is, is at work.

But, we might finally object, if the work is indeed to bring thingness cogently into the Open, must it not then itself—and indeed before its own creation and for the sake of its creation—have been brought into a relation with the things of earth, with nature? Someone who was bound to know what he was talking about, Albrecht Dürer, did after all make the well-known remark: "For in truth, art lies hidden within nature; he who can wrest it from her, has it." "Wrest" here means to draw out the rift and to draw the design with the drawing-pen on the drawing-board.* But we at once raise the counterquestion: how can the rift-design be drawn out if it is not brought into the Open by the creative sketch as a rift, which is to say, brought out beforehand as a conflict of measure and unmeasure? True, there lies hidden in nature a rift-design, a measure and a boundary and, tied to it, a capacity for bringing forth—that is, art. But it is equally certain that this art hidden in nature becomes manifest only through the work, because it lies originally in the work.

The trouble we are taking over the reality of the work is intended as spadework for discovering art and the nature of art in the actual work. The question concerning the nature of art, the way toward knowledge of it, is first to be placed on a firm ground again. The answer to the question, like every genuine answer, is only the final result of the last step in a long series

---

* "Reissen heisst hier Herausholen des Risses und den Riss reissen mit der Reissfeder auf dem Reissbrett."

of questions. Each answer remains in force as an answer only as long as it is rooted in questioning.

The reality of the work has become not only clearer for us in the light of its work-being, but also essentially richer. The pre-servers of a work belong to its createdness with an essentiality equal to that of the creators. But it is the work that makes the creators possible in their nature, and that by its own nature is in need of preservers. If art is the origin of the work, this means that art lets those who naturally belong together at work, the creator and the preserver, originate, each in his own nature. What, however, is art itself that we call it rightly an origin?

In the work, the happening of truth is at work and, indeed, at work according to the manner of a work. Accordingly the nature of art was defined to begin with as the setting-into-work of truth. Yet this definition is intentionally ambiguous. It says on the one hand: art is the fixing in place of a self-establishing truth in the figure. This happens in creation as the bringing forth of the unconcealedness of what is. Setting-into-work, however, also means: the bringing of work-being into move-ment and happening. This happens as preservation. Thus art is: the creative preserving of truth in the work. *Art then is the becoming and happening of truth.* Does truth, then, arise out of nothing? It does indeed if by nothing is meant the mere not of that which is, and if we here think of that which is as an object present in the ordinary way, which thereafter comes to light and is challenged by the existence of the work as only presumptively a true being. Truth is never gathered from ob-jects that are present and ordinary. Rather, the opening up of the Open, and the clearing of what is, happens only as the openness is projected, sketched out, that makes its advent in thrownness.*

---

* Thrownness, *Geworfenheit,* is understood in *Being and Time* as an exis-tential characteristic of *Dasein,* human being, its thatness, its "that it is," and it refers to the facticity of human being's being handed over to itself, its being on its own responsibility; as long as human being is what it is, it

Truth, as the clearing and concealing of what is, happens in being composed, as a poet composes a poem. *All art,* as the letting happen of the advent of the truth of what is, is, as such, *essentially poetry.* The nature of art, on which both the art work and the artist depend, is the setting-itself-into-work of truth. It is due to art's poetic nature that, in the midst of what is, art breaks open an open place, in whose openness everything is other than usual. By virtue of the projected sketch set into the work of the unconcealedness of what is, which casts itself toward us, everything ordinary and hitherto existing becomes an unbeing. This unbeing has lost the capacity to give and keep being as measure. The curious fact here is that the work in no way affects hitherto existing entities by causal connections. The working of the work does not consist in the taking effect of a cause. It lies in a change, happening from out of the work, of the unconcealedness of what is, and this means, of Being.

Poetry, however, is not an aimless imagining of whimsicalities and not a flight of mere notions and fancies into the realm of the unreal. What poetry, as illuminating projection, unfolds of unconcealedness and projects ahead into the design of the figure, is the Open which poetry lets happen, and indeed in such a way that only now, in the midst of beings, the Open brings beings to shine and ring out. If we fix our vision on the nature of the work and its connection with the happening of the truth of what is, it becomes questionable whether the nature of poetry, and this means at the same time the nature of pro-

---

is thrown, cast, "im Wurf." Projection, *Entwurf,* on the other hand, is a second existential character of human being, referring to its driving forward toward its own possibility of being. It takes the form of understanding, which the author speaks of as the mode of being of human being in which human being *is* in its possibilities *as* possibilities. It is not the mere having of a preconceived plan, but is the projecting of possibility in human being that occurs antecedently to all plans and makes planning possible. Human being is both thrown and projected; it is thrown project, factical directedness toward possibilities of being.—TR.

jection, can be adequately thought of in terms of the power of imagination.

The nature of poetry, which has now been ascertained very broadly—but not on that account vaguely, may here be kept firmly in mind as something worthy of questioning, something that still has to be thought through.

If all art is in essence poetry, then the arts of architecture, painting, sculpture, and music must be traced back to poesy. That is pure arbitrariness. It certainly is, as long as we mean that those arts are varieties of the art of language, if it is permissible to characterize poesy by that easily misinterpretable title. But poesy is only one mode of the lighting projection of truth, i.e., of poetic composition in this wider sense. Nevertheless, the linguistic work, the poem in the narrower sense, has a privileged position in the domain of the arts.

To see this, only the right concept of language is needed. In the current view, language is held to be a kind of communication. It serves for verbal exchange and agreement, and in general for communicating. But language is not only and not primarily an audible and written expression of what is to be communicated. It not only puts forth in words and statements what is overtly or covertly intended to be communicated; language alone brings what is, as something that is, into the Open for the first time. Where there is no language, as in the being of stone, plant, and animal, there is also no openness of what is, and consequently no openness either of that which is not and of the empty.

Language, by naming beings for the first time, first brings beings to word and to appearance. Only this naming nominates beings *to* their being *from out of* their being. Such saying is a projecting of the clearing, in which announcement is made of what it is that beings come into the Open *as*. Projecting is the release of a throw by which unconcealedness submits and infuses itself into what is as such. This projective announcement forthwith becomes a renunciation of all the dim confusion in which what is veils and withdraws itself.

Projective saying is poetry: the saying of world and earth, the saying of the arena of their conflict and thus of the place of all nearness and remoteness of the gods. Poetry is the saying of the unconcealedness of what is. Actual language at any given moment is the happening of this saying, in which a people's world historically arises for it and the earth is preserved as that which remains closed. Projective saying is saying which, in preparing the sayable, simultaneously brings the unsayable as such into a world. In such saying, the concepts of an historical people's nature, i.e., of its belonging to world history, are formed for that folk, before it.

Poetry is thought of here in so broad a sense and at the same time in such intimate unity of being with language and word, that we must leave open whether art, in all its modes from architecture to poesy, exhausts the nature of poetry.

Language itself is poetry in the essential sense. But since language is the happening in which for man beings first disclose themselves to him each time as beings, poesy—or poetry in the narrower sense—is the most original form of poetry in the essential sense. Language is not poetry because it is the primal poesy; rather, poesy takes place in language because language preserves the original nature of poetry. Building and plastic creation, on the other hand, always happen already, and happen only, in the Open of saying and naming. It is the Open that pervades and guides them. But for this very reason they remain their own ways and modes in which truth orders itself into work. They are an ever special poetizing within the clearing of what is, which has already happened unnoticed in language.

Art, as the setting-into-work of truth, is poetry. Not only the creation of the work is poetic, but equally poetic, though in its own way, is the preserving of the work; for a work is in actual effect as a work only when we remove ourselves from our commonplace routine and move into what is disclosed by the work, so as to bring our own nature itself to take a stand in the truth of what is.

The nature of art is poetry. The nature of poetry, in turn, is the founding of truth. We understand founding here in a triple sense: founding as bestowing, founding as grounding, and founding as beginning. Founding, however, is actual only in preserving. Thus to each mode of founding there corresponds a mode of preserving. We can do no more now than to present this structure of the nature of art in a few strokes, and even this only to the extent that the earlier characterization of the nature of the work offers an initial hint.

The setting-into-work of truth thrusts up the unfamiliar and extraordinary and at the same time thrusts down the ordinary and what we believe to be such. The truth that discloses itself in the work can never be proved or derived from what went before. What went before is refuted in its exclusive reality by the work. What art founds can therefore never be compensated and made up for by what is already present and available. Founding is an overflow, an endowing, a bestowal.

The poetic projection of truth that sets itself into work as figure is also never carried out in the direction of an indeterminate void. Rather, in the work, truth is thrown toward the coming preservers, that is, toward an historical group of men. What is thus cast forth is, however, never an arbitrary demand. Genuinely poetic projection is the opening up or disclosure of that into which human being as historical is already cast. This is the earth and, for an historical people, its earth, the self-closing ground on which it rests together with everything that it already is, though still hidden from itself. It is, however, its world, which prevails in virtue of the relation of human being to the unconcealedness of Being. For this reason, everything with which man is endowed must, in the projection, be drawn up from the closed ground and expressly set upon this ground. In this way the ground is first grounded as the bearing ground.

All creation, because it is such a drawing-up, is a drawing, as of water from a spring. Modern subjectivism, to be sure, immediately misinterprets creation, taking it as the self-sovereign subject's performance of genius. The founding of truth is a founding not only in the sense of free bestowal, but at the same time foundation in the sense of this ground-laying grounding. Poetic projection comes from Nothing in this respect, that it never takes its gift from the ordinary and traditional. But it never comes from Nothing in that what is projected by it is only the withheld vocation of the historical being of man itself.

Bestowing and grounding have in themselves the unmediated character of what we call a beginning. Yet this unmediated character of a beginning, the peculiarity of a leap out of the unmediable, does not exclude but rather includes the fact that the beginning prepares itself for the longest time and wholly inconspicuously. A genuine beginning, as a leap, is always a head start, in which everything to come is already leaped over, even if as something disguised. The beginning already contains the end latent within itself. A genuine beginning, however, has nothing of the neophyte character of the primitive. The primitive, because it lacks the bestowing, grounding leap and head start, is always futureless. It is not capable of releasing anything more from itself because it contains nothing more than that in which it is caught.

A beginning, on the contrary, always contains the undisclosed abundance of the unfamiliar and extraordinary, which means that it also contains strife with the familiar and ordinary. Art as poetry is founding, in the third sense of instigation of the strife of truth: founding as beginning. Always when that which is as a whole demands, as what is, itself, a grounding in openness, art attains to its historical nature as foundation. This foundation happened in the West for the first time in Greece.

What was in the future to be called Being was set into work, setting the standard. The realm of beings thus opened up was then transformed into a being in the sense of God's creation. This happened in the Middle Ages. This kind of being was again transformed at the beginning and in the course of the modern age. Beings became objects that could be controlled and seen through by calculation. At each time a new and essential world arose. At each time the openness of what is had to be established in beings themselves, by the fixing in place of truth in figure. At each time there happened unconcealedness of what is. Unconcealedness sets itself into work, a setting which is accomplished by art.

Whenever art happens—that is, whenever there is a beginning—a thrust enters history, history either begins or starts over again. History means here not a sequence in time of events of whatever sort, however important. History is the transporting of a people into its appointed task as entrance into that people's endowment.

Art is the setting-into-work of truth. In this proposition an essential ambiguity is hidden, in which truth is at once the subject and the object of the setting. But subject and object are unsuitable names here. They keep us from thinking precisely this ambiguous nature, a task that no longer belongs to this consideration. Art is historical, and as historical it is the creative preserving of truth in the work. Art happens as poetry. Poetry is founding in the triple sense of bestowing, grounding, and beginning. Art, as founding, is essentially historical. This means not only that art has a history in the external sense that in the course of time it, too, appears along with many other things, and in the process changes and passes away and offers changing aspects for historiology. Art is history in the essential sense that it grounds history.

Art lets truth originate. Art, founding preserving, is the spring that leaps to the truth of what is, in the work. To originate something by a leap, to bring something into being from out of the source of its nature in a founding leap—this is what the word origin (German *Ursprung,* literally, primal leap) means.

The origin of the work of art—that is, the origin of both the creators and the preservers, which is to say of a people's historical existence, is art. This is so because art is by nature an origin: a distinctive way in which truth comes into being, that is, becomes historical.

We inquire into the nature of art. Why do we inquire in this way? We inquire in this way in order to be able to ask more truly whether art is or is not an origin in our historical existence, whether and under what conditions it can and must be an origin.

Such reflection cannot force art and its coming-to-be. But this reflective knowledge is the preliminary and therefore indispensable preparation for the becoming of art. Only such knowledge prepares its space for art, their way for the creators, their location for the preservers.

In such knowledge, which can only grow slowly, the question is decided whether art can be an origin and then must be a head start, or whether it is to remain a mere appendix and then can only be carried along as a routine cultural phenomenon.

Are we in our existence historically at the origin? Do we know, which means do we give heed to, the nature of the origin? Or, in our relation to art, do we still merely make appeal to a cultivated acquaintance with the past?

For this either-or and its decision there is an infallible sign. Hölderlin, the poet—whose work still confronts the Germans as a test to be stood—named it in saying:

> Schwer verlässt
> was nahe dem Ursprung wohnet, den Ort.

> Reluctantly
> that which dwells near its origin departs.
> —"The Journey," verses 18–19

Epilogue

The foregoing reflections are concerned with the riddle of art, the riddle that art itself is. They are far from claiming to solve the riddle. The task is to see the riddle.

Almost from the time when specialized thinking about art and the artist began, this thought was called aesthetic. Aesthetics takes the work of art as an object, the object of *aisthesis,* of sensuous apprehension in the wide sense. Today we call this apprehension experience. The way in which man experiences art is supposed to give information about its nature. Experience is the source that is standard not only for art appreciation and enjoyment, but also for artistic creation. Everything is an experience. Yet perhaps experience is the element in which art dies. The dying occurs so slowly that it takes a few centuries.

To be sure, people speak of immortal works of art and of art as an eternal value. Speaking this way means using that language which does not trouble with precision in all essential matters, for fear that in the end to be precise would call for—thinking. And is there any greater fear today than that of thinking? Does this talk about immortal works and the eternal value of art have any content or substance? Or are these merely the half-baked clichés of an age when great art, together with its nature, has departed from among men?

In the most comprehensive reflection on the nature of art that the West possesses—comprehensive because it stems from metaphysics—namely Hegel's *Vorlesungen über die Asthetik,* the following propositions occur:

Art no longer counts for us as the highest manner in which truth obtains existence for itself.

One may well hope that art will continue to advance and perfect itself, but its form has ceased to be the highest need of the spirit.

In all these relationships art is and remains for us, on the side of its highest vocation, something past.*

The judgment that Hegel passes in these statements cannot be evaded by pointing out that since Hegel's lectures in aesthetics were given for the last time during the winter of 1828–29 at the University of Berlin, we have seen the rise of many new art works and new art movements. Hegel never meant to deny this possibility. But the question remains: is art still an essential and necessary way in which that truth happens which is decisive for our historical existence, or is art no longer of this character? If, however, it is such no longer, then there remains the question why this is so. The truth of Hegel's judgment has not yet been decided; for behind this verdict there stands Western thought since the Greeks, which thought corresponds to a truth of beings that has already happened. Decision upon the judgment will be made, when it is made, from and about this truth of what is. Until then the judgment remains in force. But for that very reason the question is necessary whether the truth that the judgment declares is final and conclusive and what follows if it is.

Such questions, which solicit us more or less definitely, can be asked only after we have first taken into consideration the nature of art. We attempt to take a few steps by posing the question of the origin of the art work. The problem is to bring to view the work-character of the work. What the word "origin" here means is thought by way of the nature of truth.

The truth of which we have spoken does not coincide with that which is generally recognized under the name and assigned

---

* In the original pagination of the *Vorlesungen,* which is repeated in the Jubiläum edition edited by H. Glockner (Stuttgart, 1953), these passages occur at X, 1, 134; 135; 16. All are in vol. 12 of this edition.—Tr.

to cognition and science as a quality in order to distinguish from it the beautiful and the good, which function as names for the values of nontheoretical activities.

Truth is the unconcealedness of that which is as something that is. Truth is the truth of Being. Beauty does not occur alongside and apart from this truth. When truth sets itself into the work, it appears. Appearance—as this being of truth in the work and as work—is beauty. Thus the beautiful belongs to the advent of truth, truth's taking of its place. It does not exist merely relative to pleasure and purely as its object. The beautiful does lie in form, but only because the *forma* once took its light from Being as the isness of what is. Being at that time made its advent as *eidos*. The *idea* fits itself into the *morphe*. The *sunolon*, the unitary whole of *morphe* and *hule*, namely the *ergon*, *is* in the manner of *energeia*. This mode of presence becomes the *actualitas* of the *ens actu*. The *actualitas* becomes reality. Reality becomes objectivity. Objectivity becomes experience. In the way in which, for the world determined by the West, that which is, is as the real, there is concealed a peculiar confluence of beauty with truth. The history of the nature of Western art corresponds to the change of the nature of truth. This is no more intelligible in terms of beauty taken for itself than it is in terms of experience, supposing that the metaphysical concept of art reaches to art's nature.

Addendum

On pages 64 and 72 a real difficulty will force itself on the attentive reader: it looks as if the remarks about the "fixing in place of truth" and the "letting happen of the advent of truth" could never be brought into accord. For "fixing in place" implies a willing which blocks and thus prevents the advent of truth. In *letting*-happen on the other hand, there is manifested a compliance and thus, as it were, a nonwilling, which clears the way for the advent of truth.

The difficulty is resolved if we understand fixing in place in the sense intended throughout the entire text of the essay, above all in the key specification "setting-into-work." Also correlated with "to place" and "to set" is "to lay"; all three meanings are still intended jointly by the Latin *ponere*.

We must think of "to place" in the sense of *thesis*. Thus on page 61 the statement is made, "Setting and taking possession are here everywhere (!) drawn from the Greek sense of *thesis*, which means a setting up in the unconcealed." The Greek "setting" means placing, as for instance, letting a statue be set up. It means laying, laying down an oblation. Placing and laying have the sense of bringing *here* into the unconcealed, bringing *forth* into what is present, that is, letting or causing to lie forth. Setting and placing here never mean the modern concept of the summoning of things to be placed over against the self (the ego-subject). The standing of the statue (i.e., the presence of the radiance facing us) is different from the standing of what

stands over against us in the sense of the object. "Standing"—
(cf. p. 36)—is the constancy of the showing or shining. By
contrast, thesis, antithesis, and synthesis in the dialectic of Kant
and German idealism mean a placing or putting within the
sphere of subjectivity of consciousness. Accordingly, Hegel—
correctly in terms of his position—interpreted the Greek *thesis*
in the sense of the immediate positing of the object. Setting in
this sense, therefore, is for him still untrue, because it is not
yet mediated by antithesis and synthesis. (Cf. "Hegel und die
Griechen" in the *Festschrift* for H. G. Gadamer, 1960.)

But if, in the context of our essay on the work of art, we
keep in mind the Greek sense of *thesis*—to let lie forth in its
radiance and presence—then the "fix" in "fix in place" can
never have the sense of rigid, motionless, and secure.

"Fixed" means outlined, admitted into the boundary (*peras*),
brought into the outline—(cf. p. 63). The boundary in the
Greek sense does not block off; rather, being itself brought
forth, it first brings to its radiance what is present. Boundary
sets free into the unconcealed; by its contour in the Greek light
the mountain stands in its towering and repose. The boundary
that fixes and consolidates is in this repose—repose in the fullness of motion—all this holds of the work in the Greek sense
of *ergon;* this work's "being" is *energeia,* which gathers in-
finitely more movement within itself than do the modern "energies."

Thus the "fixing in place" of truth, rightly understood, can
never run counter to the "letting happen." For one thing, this
"letting" is nothing passive but a doing in the highest degree
(cf. "Wissenschaft und Besinnung" in *Vorträge und Aufsätze,*
p. 49)* in the sense of *thesis,* a "working" and "willing"

---

* The reference is to a discussion of the German *Tun,* doing, which points
to the core of its meaning as a laying forth, placing here, bringing here and
bringing forth—"working," in the sense either of something bringing itself
forth out of itself into presence or of man performing the bringing here and
bringing forth of something. Both are a way in which something that is present presences.—Tr.

which in the present essay—(p. 67) is characterized as the "existing human being's entrance into and compliance with the unconcealedness of Being." For another thing, the "happen" in the letting happen of truth is the movement that prevails in the clearing *and* concealing or more precisely in their union, that is to say, the movement of the lighting of self-concealment as such, from which again all self-lighting stems. What is more, this "movement" even requires a fixing in place in the sense of a bringing forth, where the bringing is to be understood in the sense given it on page 62, in that the creative bringing forth "is rather a receiving and an incorporating of a relation to unconcealedness."

In accordance with what has so far been explained, the meaning of the noun *"Ge-Stell,"* frame, framing, framework, used on page 64, is thus defined: the gathering of the bringing-forth, of the letting-come-forth-here into the rift-design as bounding outline (*peras*). The Greek sense of *morphe* as figure, *Gestalt,* is made clear by *"Ge-Stell,"* "framing," so understood. Now the word "Ge-Stell," frame, which we used in later writings as the explicit key expression for the nature of modern technology, was indeed conceived in reference to that sense of frame (*not* in reference to such other senses as bookshelf or montage, which it also has). That context is essential, because related to the destiny of Being. Framing, as the nature of modern technology, derives from the Greek way of experiencing letting-lie-forth, *logos,* from the Greek *poiesis* and *thesis.* In setting up the frame, the framework—which now means in commandeering everything into assured availability—there sounds the claim of the *ratio reddenda,* i.e., of the *logon dido-nai,* but in such a way that today this claim that is made in framing takes control of the absolute, and the process of representation—of *Vor-stellen* or putting forth—takes form, on the basis of the Greek perception, as making secure, fixing in place.

When we hear the words "fix in place" and "framing" or "framework" in "The Origin of the Work of Art," we must, on the one hand, put out of mind the modern meaning of placing or framing, and yet at the same time we must not fail to note that, and in what way, the Being that defines the modern period—Being as framing, framework—stems from the Western destiny of Being and has not been thought *up* by philosophers but rather thought to thinking men (cf. *Vorträge und Aufsätze,* pp. 28 and 49*).

It is still our burden to discuss the specifications given briefly on pages 61f. about the "establishing" and "self-establishing of truth in that which is, in beings." Here again we must avoid understanding "establish" in the modern sense and in the manner of the lecture on technology as "organize" and "finish or complete." Rather, "establishing" recalls the "impulse of truth toward the work," mentioned on page 62, the impulse that, in the midst of beings, truth should itself be in the manner of work, should itself occur as being.

* The reference to page 49 is to the conception of doing, as given in the previous note. The passage on page 28 of *Vorträge und Aufsätze* appears in the essay *"Die Frage nach der Technik."* The *"-Stell"* in *"Ge-Stell"* comes from the German "stellen," a transitive verb meaning to place, put, set, stand, arrange. *"Ge-Stell,"* if taken literally, would then be the collective name for all sorts of placing, putting, setting, arranging, ordering, or in general, putting in place. Heidegger pushes this collective reading further, in the light of his interpretation of early Greek language and thought, his general concept of truth and the history of Being, and his view of the work of Being in summoning and gathering men to their destiny. The gathering agent today is the call that challenges men to put everything that discloses itself into the position of stock, resource, material for technological processing. For this call, this gathering power, Heidegger makes use of this collective word which expresses the gathering of all forms of ordering things as resources—*das Ge-Stell,* the collective unity of all the putting, placing, setting, standing, arraying, arranging that goes into modern technology and the life oriented to it. The *"stellen,"* the setting, placing, in the word, derives from an older mode, that of *poiesis,* which lets what is present come forth into unconcealedness, as in the setting up of a statue in the temple precinct; yet both the modern technological setting up of things as resources and this ancient poetic setting up of them as bearing their world are modes of unconcealing, of truth as *aletheia.* They are not mere inventions of men or mere doings of men, but are phases in the history of the destiny of Being and of man in his historical situation in relation to Being. Contemporary man's technological "things" bear his technological "world" in their own distorted way—distorting man's earth, his heaven, his divinities, and, in the end, himself and his mortality. —Tr.

If we recollect how truth as unconcealedness of beings means nothing but the presence of beings as such, that is, *Being*—see page 72—then talk about the self-establishing of truth, that is, of Being, in all that is, touches on the problem of the ontological difference.* For this reason there is the note of caution on page 61 of "The Origin of the Work of Art": "In referring to this self-establishing of openness in the Open, thinking touches on a sphere that cannot yet be explicated here." The whole essay, "The Origin of the Work of Art," deliberately yet tacitly moves on the path of the question of the nature of Being. Reflection on what *art* may be is completely and decidedly determined only in regard to the question of *Being*. Art is considered neither an area of cultural achievement nor an appearance of spirit; it belongs to the *disclosure of appropriation* by way of which the "meaning of Being" (cf. *Being and Time*) can alone be defined. What art may be is one of the questions to which no answers are given in the essay. What gives the impression of such an answer are directions for questioning. (Cf. the first sentences of the Epilogue.)

Among these directions there are two *important hints,* on pages 71 and 77. In both places mention is made of an "ambiguity." On page 77 an "essential ambiguity" is noted in regard to the definition of art as "the setting-into-work of truth." In this ambiguity, truth is "subject" on the one hand and "object" on the other. *Both* descriptions remain "unsuitable." If truth is the "subject," then the definition "the setting-into-work of truth" means: "truth's setting itself into work"—compare pages 71 and 36. Art is then conceived in terms of disclosive appropriation. Being, however, is a call to man and is not without man. Accordingly, art is at the same time defined as the setting-into-work of truth, where truth *now* is "object" and art is human creating and preserving.

* Cf. *Identität und Differenz* (1957), pp. 37 ff.; English *Identity and Difference,* trans. by Joan Stambaugh (New York: Harper & Row, 1969), pp. 50 ff., 116 ff.

Within the *human* relation to art there results the second ambiguity of the setting-into-work of truth, which on page 71 was called creation and preservation. According to pages 70 and 57f. the art *work* and the art*ist* rest "especially" in what goes on in art. In the heading "the setting-into-work of truth," in which it remains undecided but decid*able* who does the setting or in what way it occurs, there is concealed *the relation of Being and human being,* a relation which is unsuitably conceived even in this version—a distressing difficulty, which has been clear to me since *Being and Time* and has since been expressed in a variety of versions (cf., finally, "Zur Seinsfrage" and the present essay, p. 61, "Only this much should be noted, that . . . .").

The problematic context that prevails here then comes together at the proper place in the discussion, where the nature of language and of poetry is touched on, all this again only in regard to the belonging together of Being and Saying.

There is an unavoidable necessity for the reader, who naturally comes to the essay from without, to refrain at first and for a long time from perceiving and interpreting the facts of the case in terms of the reticent domain that is the source of what has to be thought. For the author himself, however, there remains the pressing need of speaking each time in the language most opportune for each of the various stations on his way.

WHAT ARE POETS FOR?

WHAT ARE POETS FOR?

". . . and what are poets for in a destitute time?" asks Hölder-lin's elegy "Bread and Wine." We hardly understand the question today. How, then, shall we grasp the answer that Hölderlin gives?

". . . and what are poets for in a destitute time?" The word "time" here means the era to which we ourselves still belong. For Hölderlin's historical experience, the appearance and sacri-ficial death of Christ mark the beginning of the end of the day of the gods. Night is falling. Ever since the "united three"— Herakles, Dionysos, and Christ—have left the world, the evening of the world's age has been declining toward its night. The world's night is spreading its darkness. The era is defined by the god's failure to arrive, by the "default of God." But the default of God which Hölderlin experienced does not deny that the Christian relationship with God lives on in individuals and in the churches; still less does it assess this relationship negatively. The default of God means that no god any longer gathers men and things unto himself, visibly and unequivocally, and by such gathering disposes the world's history and man's sojourn in it. The default of God forebodes something even grimmer, however. Not only have the gods and the god fled, but the divine radiance has become extinguished in the world's history. The time of the world's night is the destitute time, because it becomes ever more destitute. It has already grown so destitute, it can no longer discern the default of God as a default.

Because of this default, there fails to appear for the world the ground that grounds it. The word for abyss—*Abgrund*—originally means the soil and ground toward which, because it is undermost, a thing tends downward. But in what follows we shall think of the *Ab-* as the complete absence of the ground. The ground is the soil in which to strike root and to stand. The age for which the ground fails to come, hangs in the abyss. Assuming that a turn still remains open for this destitute time at all, it can come some day only if the world turns about fundamentally—and that now means, unequivocally: if it turns away from the abyss. In the age of the world's night, the abyss of the world must be experienced and endured. But for this it is necessary that there be those who reach into the abyss.

The turning of the age does not take place by some new god, or the old one renewed, bursting into the world from ambush at some time or other. Where would he turn on his return if men had not first prepared an abode for him? How could there ever be for the god an abode fit for a god, if a divine radiance did not first begin to shine in everything that is?

The gods who "were once there," "return" only at the "right time"—that is, when there has been a turn among men in the right place, in the right way. For this reason Hölderlin, in the unfinished hymn "Mnemosyne," written soon after the elegy "Bread and Wine," writes (IV, 225):

> . . . The heavenly powers
> Cannot do all things. It is the mortals
> Who reach sooner into the abyss. So the turn is
> With these. Long is
> The time, but the true comes into
> Its own.

Long is the destitute time of the world's night. To begin with, this requires a long time to reach to its middle. At this night's midnight, the destitution of the time is greatest. Then the destitute time is no longer able even to experience its own destitution. That inability, by which even the destitution of the destitute state is obscured, is the time's absolutely destitute character. The destitution is wholly obscured, in that it now appears as nothing more than the need that wants to be met. Yet we must think of the world's night as a destiny that takes place this side of pessimism and optimism. Perhaps the world's night is now approaching its midnight. Perhaps the world's time is now becoming the completely destitute time. But also perhaps not, not yet, not even yet, despite the immeasurable need, despite all suffering, despite nameless sorrow, despite the growing and spreading peacelessness, despite the mounting confusion. Long is the time because even terror, taken by itself as a ground for turning, is powerless as long as there is no turn with mortal men. But there is a turn with mortals when these find the way to their own nature. That nature lies in this, that mortals reach into the abyss sooner than the heavenly powers. Mortals, when we think of their nature, remain closer to that absence because they are touched by presence, the ancient name of Being. But because presence conceals itself at the same time, it is itself already absence. Thus the abyss holds and remarks everything. In his hymn "The Titans" Hölderlin says of the "abyss" that it is "all-perceiving." He among mortals who must, sooner than other mortals and otherwise than they, reach into the abyss, comes to know the marks that the abyss remarks. For the poet, these are the traces of the fugitive gods. In Hölderlin's experience, Dionysos the wine-god brings this trace down to the god-less amidst the darkness of their world's night. For in the vine and in its fruit, the god of wine guards the being toward one another of earth and sky as the site of the wedding feast of men and gods. Only within reach of this site, if anywhere, can traces of the fugitive gods still remain for god-less men.

". . . and what are poets for in a destitute time?"

Hölderlin shyly puts the answer into the mouth of his poet-friend Heinse, whom he addresses in the elegy:

"But they are, you say, like the wine-god's holy priests,
Who fared from land to land in holy night."

Poets are the mortals who, singing earnestly of the wine-god, sense the trace of the fugitive gods, stay on the gods' tracks, and so trace for their kindred mortals the way toward the turning. The ether, however, in which alone the gods are gods, is their godhead. The element of this ether, that within which even the godhead itself is still present, is the holy. The element of the ether for the coming of the fugitive gods, the holy, is the track of the fugitive gods. But who has the power to sense, to trace such a track? Traces are often inconspicuous, and are always the legacy of a directive that is barely divined. To be a poet in a destitute time means: to attend, singing, to the trace of the fugitive gods. This is why the poet in the time of the world's night utters the holy. This is why, in Hölderlin's language, the world's night is the holy night.

It is a necessary part of the poet's nature that, before he can be truly a poet in such an age, the time's destitution must have made the whole being and vocation of the poet a poetic question for him. Hence "poets in a destitute time" must especially gather in poetry the nature of poetry. Where that happens we may assume poets to exist who are on the way to the destiny of the world's age. We others must learn to listen to what *these* poets say—assuming that, in regard to the time that conceals Being because it shelters it, we do not deceive ourselves through reckoning time merely in terms of that which is by dissecting that which is.

The closer the world's night draws toward midnight, the more exclusively does the destitute prevail, in such a way that it withdraws its very nature and presence. Not only is the holy lost as the track toward the godhead; even the traces leading to that lost track are well-nigh obliterated. The more obscure the traces become the less can a single mortal, reaching into the abyss, attend there to intimations and signs. It is then all the more strictly true that each man gets farthest if he goes only as far as he can go along the way allotted to him. The third stanza of the same elegy that raises the question—"What are poets for in a destitute time?"—pronounces the law that rules over its poets:

> One thing stands firm: whether it be near noon
> Or close to midnight, a measure ever endures,
> Common to all; yet to each his own is allotted, too,
> Each of us goes toward and reaches the place that
>   he can.

In his letter to Boehlendorf of December 2, 1802 Hölderlin writes: ". . . and the philosophical light around my window is now my joy; may I be able to keep on as I have thus far!"

The poet thinks his way into the locality defined by that lightening of Being which has reached its characteristic shape as the realm of Western metaphysics in its self-completion. Hölderlin's thinking poetry has had a share in giving its shape to this realm of poetic thinking. His composing dwells in this locality as intimately as no other poetic composition of his time. The locality to which Hölderlin came is a manifestness of Being, a manifestness which itself belongs to the destiny of Being and which, out of that destiny, is intended for the poet.

But this manifestness of Being within metaphysics as completed may even be at the same time the extreme oblivion of Being. Suppose, however, that this oblivion were the hidden nature of the destituteness of what is destitute in the time. There would indeed be no time then for an aesthetic flight to Hölderlin's poetry. There would then be no moment in which to make a contrived myth out of the figure of the poet. There would then be no occasion to misuse his poetry as a rich source for a philosophy. But there would be, and there is, the sole necessity, by thinking our way soberly into what his poetry says, to come to learn what is unspoken. That is the course of the history of Being. If we reach and enter that course, it will lead thinking into a dialogue with poetry, a dialogue that is of the history of Being. Scholars of literary history inevitably consider that dialogue to be an unscientific violation of what such scholarship takes to be the facts. Philosophers consider the dialogue to be a helpless aberration into fantasy. But destiny pursues its course untroubled by all that.

Do we moderns encounter a modern poet on this course? Do we encounter that very poet who today is often and hastily dragged into the vicinity of thinking, and covered up with much half-baked philosophy? However, we must ask this question more clearly, with the appropriate rigor.

Is Rainer Maria Rilke a poet in a destitute time? How is his poetry related to the destitution of the time? How deeply does it reach into the abyss? Where does the poet get to, assuming he goes where he can go?

Rilke's valid poetry concentrates and solidifies itself, patiently assembled, in the two slim volumes *Duino Elegies* and *Sonnets to Orpheus*.* The long way leading to the poetry is itself one that inquires poetically. Along the way Rilke comes to realize the destitution of the time more clearly. The time remains destitute not only because God is dead, but because mortals are hardly aware and capable even of their own mortality. Mortals have not yet come into ownership of their own nature. Death withdraws into the enigmatic. The mystery of pain remains veiled. Love has not been learned. But the mortals *are*. They are, in that there is language. Song still lingers over their destitute land. The singer's word still keeps to the trace of the holy. The song in the *Sonnets to Orpheus* (Part I, 19) says it:

* *Duineser Elegien*. Leipzig: Insel-Verlag, 1923. *Die Sonette an Orpheus*. Leipzig: Insel-Verlag, 1923.—Tr.

Though swiftly the world converts,
like cloud-shapes' upheaval,
everything perfect reverts
to the primeval.

Over the change abounding
farther and freer
your preluding song keeps sounding
God with the lyre.

Suffering is not discerned,
neither has love been learned,
and what removes us in death,
nothing unveils.
Only the song's high breath
hallows and hails.

Meanwhile, even the trace of the holy has become unrecognizable. It remains undecided whether we still experience the holy as the track leading to the godhead of the divine, or whether we now encounter no more than a trace of the holy. It remains unclear what the track leading to the trace might be. It remains in question how such a track might show itself to us.

The time is destitute because it lacks the unconcealedness of the nature of pain, death, and love. This destitution is itself destitute because that realm of being withdraws within which pain and death and love belong together. Concealedness exists inasmuch as the realm in which they belong together is the abyss of Being. But the song still remains which names the land over which it sings. What is the song itself? How is a mortal capable of it? Whence does it sing? How far does it reach into the abyss?

In order to fathom whether and in what way Rilke is a poet in a destitute time, and in order to know, then, what poets are for, we must try to stake out a few markers along the path to the abyss. We shall use as our markers some of the basic words of Rilke's valid poetry. They can be understood only in the context of the realm from which they were spoken. That realm is the truth of particular beings, as it has developed since the completion of Western metaphysics by Nietzsche. Rilke has in his own way poetically experienced and endured the unconceal-edness of beings which was shaped by that completion. Let us observe how beings as such and as a whole show themselves to Rilke. In order to bring this realm into view, we shall give close attention to a poem that originated within the horizon of Rilke's perfected poetry, though later in point of time.

We are unprepared for the interpretation of the elegies and the sonnets, since the realm from which they speak, in its meta-physical constitution and unity, has not yet been sufficiently thought out in terms of the nature of metaphysics. Such think-ing remains difficult, for two reasons. For one thing, because Rilke's poetry does not come up to Hölderlin's in its rank and position in the course of the history of Being. For another, because we barely know the nature of metaphysics and are not experienced travelers in the land of the saying of Being.

We are not only unprepared for an interpretation of the elegies and the sonnets, but also we have no right to it, because the realm in which the dialogue between poetry and thinking goes on can be discovered, reached, and explored in thought only slowly. Who today would presume to claim that he is at home with the nature of poetry as well as with the nature of thinking and, in addition, strong enough to bring the nature of the two into the most extreme discord and so to establish their concord?

Rilke did not himself publish the poem discussed below. It may be found on page 118 of the volume *Gesammelte Gedichte* which appeared in 1934, and on page 90 of the collection *Späte Gedichte* published in 1935. The poem bears no title. Rilke wrote it down in June 1924. In a letter to Clara Rilke from Muzot, August 15, 1924, the poet writes: "But I have not been so remiss and sluggish in *all* directions, luckily, Baron

Lucius received his beautiful *Malte* even *before* my departure in June; his note of thanks has long been waiting, ready to be sent on to you. I also enclose the improvised verses which I inscribed for him in the first volume of the handsome leather edition."*

According to a note by the editors of the *Briefe aus Muzot* (p. 404), the improvised verses here referred to by Rilke make up the following poem:

1   As Nature gives the other creatures over
2   to the venture of their dim delight
3   and in soil and branchwork grants none special cover,
4   so too our being's pristine ground settles our plight;
5   we are no dearer to it; it ventures us.
6   Except that we, more eager than plant or beast,
7   go *with* this venture, will it, adventurous
8   more sometimes than Life itself is, more daring
9   by a breath (and not in the least
10   from selfishness) . . . . There, outside all caring,
11   this creates for us a safety—just there,
12   where the pure forces' gravity rules; in the end,
13   it is our unshieldedness on which we depend,
14   and that, when we saw it threaten, we turned it
15   so into the Open that, in widest orbit somewhere,
16   where the Law touches us, we may affirm it.

Rilke calls this poem "improvised verses." But its unforeseen character opens for us a perspective in which we are able to think Rilke's poetry more clearly. True, at this moment in the world's history we have first to learn that the making of poetry,

* *Briefe aus Muzot,* edited by Ruth Sieber-Rilke and Carl Sieber. Leipzig: Insel-Verlag 1936 (c. 1935). *Gesammelte Gedichte,* 4 vols. Leipzig: Insel-Verlag, 1930–1934 (Bd. 4: Leipzig: Pöschel & Trepete, 1934). *Späte Gedichte.* Leipzig: Insel-Verlag, 1934.—TR.

too, is a matter of thinking. Let us take the poem as an exercise in poetic self-reflection.

The poem's structure is simple. Its articulation is clear, yielding four parts: verses 1–5; verses 6–10; verses 10–12; and verses 12–16.* The "so too our" in line 4 corresponds to the beginning, "As Nature." The "Except that" in line 6 refers back to this "our." This "Except that" restricts, but in the way in which a distinguished rank restricts its bearer. The distinction is identified in lines 6–10. Lines 10–12 state what the distinction is capable of. What it actually consists of is thought out in lines 12–16.

Through the "As Nature . . . so too our" at the beginning, man's being enters into the theme of the poem. The comparison contrasts human being with all other creatures. They are the living beings, plant and animal. The opening of the eighth Duino Elegy, making the same comparison, calls all beings "the Creature."

A comparison places different things in an identical setting to make the difference visible. The different things, plant and beast on the one hand and man on the other, are identical in that they come to unite within the same. This same is the relation which they have, as beings, to their ground. The ground of beings is Nature. The ground of man is not only of a kind identical with that of plant and beast. The ground is the same for both. It is Nature, as "full Nature" (*Sonnets to Orpheus,* II, 13).

We must here think of Nature in the broad and essential sense in which Leibniz uses the word *Natura* capitalized. It means the Being of beings. Being occurs as the *vis primitiva activa.* This is the incipient power gathering everything to itself, which in this manner releases every being to its own self. The Being of beings is the will. The will is the self-concentrating

---

* In the German text the verse numbers vary slightly from these, due to differences between the original poem and the translated version. The numbers for the original are: 1–5; 5–9; 10–11; 12–16.—TR.

gathering of every *ens* unto itself. Every being, as a being, is in the will. It *is* as something willed. This should be taken as saying: that which is, is not first and only as something willed; rather, insofar as it is, it is itself in the mode of will. Only by virtue of being willed is each being that which, in its own way, does the willing in the will.

What Rilke calls Nature is not contrasted with history. Above all, it is not intended as the subject matter of natural science. Nor is Nature opposed to art. It is the ground for history and art and nature in the narrower sense. In the word Nature as used here, there echoes still the earlier word *phusis*, equated also with *zoe,* which we translate "life." In early thought, however, the nature of life is not conceived in biological terms, but as the *phusis,* that which arises. In line 8 of our poem, "Nature" is also called "Life." Nature, Life here designate Being in the sense of all beings as a whole. In a note of 1885/86, Nietzsche once wrote: "Being—we have no idea of it other than 'living.'— How can anything dead 'be'?"*

Rilke calls Nature the *Urgrund,* the pristine ground, because it is the ground of those beings that we ourselves are. This suggests that man reaches more deeply into the ground of beings than do other beings. The ground of beings has since ancient times been called Being. The relation of Being which grounds to the beings that are grounded, is identical for man on the one hand, plant and beast on the other. It consists in this, that Being each time "gives" particular beings "over to venture." Being lets beings loose into the daring venture. This release, flinging them loose, is the real daring. The Being of beings is this relation of the flinging loose to beings. Whoever is in being at a given time is what is being ventured. Being is the venture pure and simple. It ventures us, us humans. It ventures the living

---

* Friedrich Nietzsche. *Der Wille Zur Macht.* In: *Nietzsches Werke.* 2 Abt. Bd. XV. *Nachgelassene Werke. Ecce Homo* und *Der Wille Zur Macht.* 1. u. 2. Buch. Leipzig, Kröner, 1922. Cf. also Nietzsche's *Werke,* edited by Karl Schlechta. Munich: Carl Hauser, 1956. Band 3, page 483.—TR.

beings. The particular being is, insofar as it remains what has ever and always been ventured. But the particular being is ventured into Being, that is, into a daring. Therefore, beings hazard themselves, are given over to venture. Beings are, by going with the venture to which they are given over. The Being of beings is the venture. This venture resides in the will which, since Leibniz, announces itself more clearly as the Being of beings that is revealed in metaphysics. We must not think of will here as the abstract generalization of willing understood in psychological terms. Rather, the human willing that is experienced metaphysically remains only the willed counterpart of will as the Being of beings. Rilke, in representing Nature as the venture, thinks of it metaphysically in terms of the nature of will. This nature of will still conceals itself, both in the will to power and in the will as venture. The will exists as the will to will.

The poem makes no direct statement about the ground of all beings, that is, about Being as the venture pure and simple. But if Being as venture is the relation of flinging loose, and thus retains in the flinging even what has been ventured, then the poem tells us something indirectly about the venture by speaking of what has been ventured.

Nature ventures living beings, and "grants none special cover." Likewise, we men who have been ventured are "no dearer" to the daring that ventures us. The two imply: venture includes flinging into danger. To dare is to risk the game. Heraclitus (Fragment 52) thinks of Being as the aeon, the world's age, and of the aeon in turn as a child's game: *Aion pais esti paizon, pesseuon • paidos he basileie.* ("Time is a child playing, playing draughts; the kingship is a child's.") If that which has been flung were to remain out of danger, it would not have been ventured. It would not be in danger if it were shielded. Words in German associated with shield are *Schutz* (protection), *Schütze* (marksman), *schützen* (to protect); they belong to *schiessen* (to shoot), as *Buck* (boss, knob), *bücken* (to bend or stoop) belong to *biegen* (to bend or bow). *Schiessen,* to shoot, means *schieben,* to thrust, e.g., to thrust home a bolt. The roof thrusts forth over the wall. In the country we still say: the peasant woman *schiesst ein,* she shoves the dough formed for baking into the oven. The shield is what is pushed before and in front of. It keeps danger from harming, even touching, the endangered being. What is shielded is entrusted to the protector, the shielder. Our older and richer language would have used words like *verlaubt, verlobt*—held dear. The unshielded, on the contrary, is "no dearer." Plant, animal, and man—insofar as they are beings at all, that is, insofar as they are ventured— agree in this, that they are not specially protected. But since they differ nonetheless in their being, there will also be a differ- ence in their unprotectedness.

As ventured, those who are not protected are nevertheless not abandoned. If they were, they would be just as little ven- tured as if they were protected. Surrendered only to annihila- tion, they would no longer hang in the balance. In the Middle Ages the word for balance, *die Wage,* still means about as much as hazard or risk. This is the situation in which matters may turn out one way or the other. That is why the apparatus which moves by tipping one way or the other is called *die Wage.* It plays and balances out. The word *Wage,* in the sense of risk and as name of the apparatus, comes from *wägen, wegen,* to make a way, that is, to go, to be in motion. *Be-wägen* means to cause to be on the way and so to bring into motion: to shake or rock, *wiegen.* What rocks is said to do so because it is able to bring the balance, *Wage,* into the play of movement, this way or that. What rocks the balance weighs down; it has weight. To weigh or throw in the balance, as in the sense of wager, means to bring into the movement of the game, to throw into the scales, to release into risk. What is so ventured is, of course, unprotected; but because it hangs in the balance, it is retained in the venture. It is upheld. Its ground keeps it safely within it. What is ventured, as something that is, is something that is willed; retained within the will, it itself remains in the mode of will, and ventures itself. What is ventured is thus careless, *sine cura, securum*—secure, safe. What is ventured can follow the venture, follow it into the unprotectedness of the ventured, only if it rests securely in the venture. The unprotectedness of what is ventured not only does not exclude, it necessarily includes, its being secure in its ground. What is ventured goes along with the venture.

Being, which holds all beings in the balance, thus always draws particular beings toward itself—toward itself as the center. Being, as the venture, holds all beings, as being ventured, in this draft. But this center of the attracting drawing withdraws at the same time from all beings. In this fashion the center gives over all beings to the venture as which they are ventured. In this gathering release, the metaphysical nature of the will, thought of in terms of Being, conceals itself. The venture—the drawing and all-mediating center of beings—is the power that lends a weight, a gravity to the ventured beings. The venture is the force of gravity. One of Rilke's late poems, entitled "The Force of Gravity," says of it:

> Center, how you draw yourself
> out of all things, regaining yourself
> even from things in flight: Center, strongest of all!
> Standing man: like a drink through thirst,
> gravity plunges through him.
> But from the sleeper there falls
> as from low-lying cloud,
> a rich rain of weight.*

In contrast with physical gravitation, of which we usually hear, the force of gravity named in this poem is the center of all beings as a whole. This is why Rilke calls it "the unheard-of center" (*Sonnets to Orpheus,* II, 28). It is the ground as the "medium" that holds one being to another in mediation and

---

* ["Schwerkraft," in Rilke, Rainer Maria, *Sämtliche Werke,* edited by the Rilke Archiv. Vol. 2, p. 179. Wiesbaden: Insel-Verlag, 1963.—Tr.]

gathers everything in the play of the venture. The unheard-of center is "the eternal playmate" in the world-game of Being. The same poem that sings of Being as the venture calls the draft that mediates here the gravity of the pure forces. The pure gravity, the unheard-of center of all daring, the eternal playmate in the game of Being, is the venture.

As the venture flings free what is ventured, it holds it at the same time in balance. The venture sets free what is ventured, in such a way indeed that it sets free what is flung free into nothing other than a drawing toward the center. Drawing this way, the venture ever and always brings the ventured toward itself in this drawing. To bring something from somewhere, to secure it, make it come—is the original meaning of the word *Bezug,* currently understood as meaning reference or relation. The drawing which, as the venture, draws and touches all beings and keeps them drawing toward itself is the *Bezug,* the draft, pure and simple. The word *Bezug* is a basic word in Rilke's valid poetry, and occurs in such combinations as "the pure *Bezug,*" "the whole," "the real," "the clearest *Bezug,*" or "the other *Bezug*" (meaning the same draft in another respect).

We only half understand Rilke's word *Bezug*—and in a case such as this that means not at all—if we understand it in the sense of reference or relation. We compound our misunderstanding if we conceive of this relation as the human ego's referring or relating itself to the object. This meaning, "referring to," is a later one in the history of language. Rilke's word *Bezug* is used in this sense as well, of course; but it does not intend it primarily, but only on the basis of its original meaning. Indeed, the expression "the whole *Bezug*" is completely unthinkable if *Bezug* is represented as mere relation. The gravity of the pure forces, the unheard-of center, the pure draft, the whole draft, full Nature, Life, the venture—they are the same.

All the names listed name what is, as such, as a whole. The common parlance of metaphysics also calls it "Being." According to the poem, Nature is to be thought of as the venture. The word "venture" here designates both the ground that dares the venture, and what is ventured as a whole. This ambiguity is not accidental, nor is it sufficient for us merely to note it. In it, the language of metaphysics speaks unequivocally.

Everything that is ventured is, as such and such a being, admitted into the whole of beings, and reposes in the ground of the whole. The given beings, of one sort or another, *are* according to the attraction by which they are held within the pull of the whole draft. The manner of attraction within the draft is the mode of the relation to the center as pure gravity. Nature therefore comes to be represented when it is said in what manner the given ventured being is drawn into the pull toward the center. According to that manner, the given being then is in the midst of beings as a whole.

Rilke likes to use the term "the Open" to designate the whole draft to which all beings, as ventured beings, are given over. It is another basic word in his poetry. In Rilke's language, "open" means something that does not block off. It does not block off because it does not set bounds. It does not set bounds because it is in itself without all bounds. The Open is the great whole of all that is unbounded. It lets the beings ventured into the pure draft draw as they are drawn, so that they variously draw on one another and draw together without encountering any bounds. Drawing as so drawn, they fuse with the boundless, the infinite. They do not dissolve into void nothingness, but they redeem themselves into the whole of the Open.

What Rilke designates by this term is not in any way defined by openness in the sense of the unconcealedness of beings that lets beings as such be present. If we attempted to interpret what Rilke has in mind as the Open in the sense of unconcealedness and what is unconcealed, we would have to say: what Rilke experiences as the Open is precisely what is closed up, unlightened, which draws on in boundlessness, so that it is incapable of encountering anything unusual, or indeed anything at all. Where something is encountered, a barrier comes into being. Where there is confinement, whatever is so barred is forced back upon itself and thus bent in upon itself. The barring twists and blocks off the relation to the Open, and makes of the relation itself a twisted one. The confinement within the boundless is established by man's representation. The oppositeness confronting him does not allow man to be directly within the Open. In a certain manner, it excludes man from the world and places him before the world—"world" meaning here all beings as a whole. In contrast, what has the character of world is the Open itself, the whole of all that is not objective. But the name "the Open," too, like the word "venture," is, as a metaphysical term, ambiguous. It signifies the whole of the unbounded drawings of the whole draft, as well as openness in the sense of a universally prevailing release from all bounds.

The Open admits. To admit does not, however, mean to grant entry and access to what is closed off, as though what is concealed had to reveal itself in order to appear as unconcealed. To admit means to draw in and to fit into the unlightened whole of the drawings of the pure draft. Admittance, as the way the Open is, has the character of an including attraction, in the manner of the gravity of the pure forces. The less ventured beings are debarred from admittance into the pure draft, the more they belong within the great whole of the Open. Rilke, accordingly, calls those beings that have been ventured directly into this great whole and there rest in the balance, the "great-accustomed things" (*Späte Gedichte,* p. 22). Man is not among them. The song that sings of this different relation of living beings and of man to the Open is the eighth of the *Duino Elegies*. The differences lie in the different degrees of consciousness. Ever since Leibniz, the distinction among beings in this respect has been current in modern metaphysics.

What Rilke thinks when he thinks the word "the Open" can be documented by a letter which he addressed in the last year of his life (February 25, 1926) to a Russian reader who had questioned him about the eighth elegy.* Rilke writes:

* Maurice Betz, *Rilke in Frankreich. Erinnerungen—Briefe—Dokumente* [Vienna, Leipzig, Zürich: Reichner, 1937.—Tr.]

You must understand the concept of the "Open," which I have tried to propose in the elegy, in *such* a way that the animal's degree of consciousness sets it into the world without the animal's placing the world over against itself at every moment (as we do); the animal is *in* the world; we stand *before it* by virtue of that peculiar turn and intensification which our consciousness has taken. [Rilke goes on,] By the "Open," therefore, I do not mean sky, air, and space; *they,* too, are "object" and thus "opaque" and closed to the man who observes and judges. The animal, the flower, presumably *is* all that, without accounting to itself, and therefore has before itself and above itself that indescribably open freedom which perhaps has its (extremely fleeting) equivalents among us only in those first moments of love when one human being sees his own vastness in another, his beloved, and in man's elevation toward God.

Plant and animal are admitted into the Open. They are "*in* the world." The "in" means: they are included and drawn, unlightened, into the drawing of the pure draft. The relation to the Open—if indeed we may still speak here of a "to"—is the unconscious one of a merely striving-drawing ramification into the whole of what is. With the heightening of consciousness, the nature of which, for modern metaphysics, is representation, the standing and the counterstanding of objects are also heightened. The higher its consciousness, the more the conscious being is excluded from the world. This is why man, in the words of Rilke's letter, is "before the world." He is not admitted into the Open. Man stands over against the world. He does not live immediately in the drift and wind of the whole draft. The passage from the letter helps us to understand the Open better, especially because Rilke here denies expressly that one may think of the Open in the sense of the openness of sky and space. Still further removed from Rilke's poetry, which remains in the shadow of a tempered Nietzschean metaphysics, is the thought of the Open in the sense of the essentially more primal lightening of Being.

All that belongs immediately within the Open is taken up by

it into the drawing of the center's attraction. Therefore, among all ventured beings, those belong most readily within the Open which are by nature benumbed, so that, in such numbness, they never strive for anything that might oppose them. The beings that exist in this way are in "dim delight."

> As Nature gives the other creatures over
> to the venture of their dim delight. . . .

"Dim" is used here in the sense of "muted": never breaking out of the draft of the unbounded drawing onward, which is untroubled by the restless relating back and forth in which conscious representation stumbles along. Dim, like the muted tone, means what rests on an underlying depth and has the nature of a bearer. "Dim" is not meant in the negative sense of "dull" or "oppressive." Rilke does not think of the dim delight as anything low and inferior. It is evidence that the great-accustomed things of Nature belong to the whole of the pure draft. Thus he can say in a late poem: "Let a flower's being be great to us" (*Späte Gedichte,* p. 89; compare *Sonnette,* II, 14). Just as the letter which we cited thinks of man and of living beings in respect of the different relation of their consciousness to the Open, so the poem speaks of the "creatures" and of "us" (humans) in respect of our different relation to the daring venture:

> Except that we, more eager than plant or beast,
> go *with* this venture . . . .

That man goes with the venture, even more than does plant or beast, could mean first that man is admitted into the Open with even less restraint than are those other beings. In fact, the "more" would have to mean just that, if the "with" were not stressed. The stress on "with" does not mean a heightening of the unrestrained going along, but signifies: for man, to go with the venture is something specifically represented and is proposed as his purpose. The venture and what it ventures, Nature, what is as a whole, the world, is brought out into prominence for man, out of the muteness of the draft that removes all barriers. But what has so been brought forward—where is it put, and by what? It is by the positioning* that belongs to representation that Nature is brought before man. Man places before himself the world as the whole of everything objective, and he places himself before the world. Man sets up the world toward himself, and delivers Nature over to himself. We must think of this placing-here, this producing, in its broad and multifarious nature. Where Nature is not satisfactory to man's representation, he reframes or redisposes it. Man produces new things where they are lacking to him. Man transposes things where they are in his way. Man interposes something between himself and things that distract him from his purpose. Man exposes things when he boosts them for sale and use. Man exposes when he sets forth his own achievement and plays up his own profession. By multifarious producing, the world is brought to stand and into position. The Open becomes an object, and is thus twisted around toward the human being. Over against the world as the object, man stations himself and sets himself up as the one who deliberately pushes through all this producing.

To put something before ourselves, propose it, in such a way that what has been proposed, having first been represented, determines all the modes of production in every respect, is a basic characteristic of the attitude which we know as willing. The willing of which we are speaking here is production, placing-here, and this in the sense of objectification purposely putting itself through, asserting itself. Plant and animal do not will because, muted in their desire, they never bring the Open before themselves as an object. They cannot go with the venture as one that is represented. Because they are admitted into the Open, the pure draft is never the objective other to themselves. Man, by contrast, goes *"with"* the venture, because he is the being who wills in the sense described:

* "Pro-positing" would be a nearer translation.—TR.

Except that we, more eager than plant or beast,
go *with* this venture, will it . . . .

The willing of which we speak here is the putting-through, the self-assertion, whose purpose *has already* posited the world as the whole of producible objects. This willing determines the nature of modern man, though at first he is not aware of its far-reaching implication, though he could not already know today by what will, as the Being of beings, this willing is willed. By such willing, modern man turns out to be the being who, in all relations to all that is, and thus in his relation to himself as well, rises up as the producer who puts through, carries out, his own self and establishes this uprising as the absolute rule. The whole objective inventory in terms of which the world appears is given over to, commended to, and thus subjected to the command of self-assertive production. Willing has in it the character of command; for purposeful self-assertion is a mode in which the attitude of the producing, and the objective character of the world, concentrate into an unconditional and therefore complete unity. In this self-concentration, the command character of the will announces itself. And through it, in the course of modern metaphysics, the long-concealed nature of the long-since existing will as the Being of beings comes to make its appearance.

Correspondingly, human willing too can be in the mode of self-assertion only by forcing everything under its dominion from the start, even before it can survey it. To such a willing, everything, beforehand and thus subsequently, turns irresistibly into material for self-assertive production. The earth and its atmosphere become raw material. Man becomes human material, which is disposed of with a view to proposed goals. The unconditioned establishment of the unconditional self-assertion by which the world is purposefully made over according to the frame of mind of man's command is a process that emerges from the hidden nature of technology. Only in modern times does this nature begin to unfold as a destiny of the truth of all beings as a whole; until now, its scattered appearances and attempts had remained incorporated within the embracing structure of the realm of culture and civilization.

Modern science and the total state, as necessary consequences of the nature of technology, are also its attendants. The same holds true of the means and forms that are set up for the organization of public opinion and of men's everyday ideas. Not only are living things technically objectivated in stock-breeding and exploitation; the attack of atomic physics on the phenomena of living matter as such is in full swing. At bottom, the essence of life is supposed to yield itself to technical production. The fact that we today, in all seriousness, discern in the results and the viewpoint of atomic physics possibilities of demonstrating human freedom and of establishing a new value theory, is a sign of the predominance of technological ideas whose development has long since been removed beyond the realm of the individual's personal views and opinions. The inherent natural power of technology shows itself further in the attempts that are being made, in adjacent areas so to speak, to master technology with the help of traditional values; but in these efforts technological means are already being employed that are not mere external forms. For generally the utilization of machinery and the manufacture of machines is not yet technology itself— it is only an instrument concordant with technology, whereby the nature of technology is established in the objective character of its raw materials. Even this, that man becomes the subject and the world the object, is a consequence of technology's nature establishing itself, and not the other way around.

When Rilke experiences the Open as the nonobjective character of full Nature, the world of willing man must stand out for him, in contrast and in a corresponding way, as what is objective. Conversely, an eye that looks out upon the integral whole of beings will receive a hint from the phenomena of rising technology, directing it toward those realms from which there could perhaps emerge a surpassing of the technical—a surpassing that would be primordially formative.

The formless formations of technological production interpose themselves before the Open of the pure draft. Things that once grew now wither quickly away. They can no longer pierce through the objectification to show their own. In a letter of November 13, 1925, Rilke writes:

> To our grandparents, a "house," a "well," a familiar steeple, even their own clothes, their cloak *still* meant infinitely more, were infinitely more intimate—almost everything a vessel in which they found something human already there, and added to its human store. Now there are intruding, from America, empty indifferent things, sham things, *dummies of life.* . . . A house, as the Americans understand it, an American apple or a winestock from over there, have *nothing* in common with the house, the fruit, the grape into which the hope and thoughtfulness of our forefathers had entered . . . .*

Yet this Americanism is itself nothing but the concentrated rebound of the willed nature of modern Europe upon a Europe for which, to be sure, in the completion of metaphysics by Nietzsche, there were thought out in advance at least some areas of the essential questionability of a world where Being begins to rule as the will to will. It is not that Americanism first surrounds us moderns with its menace; the menace of the un-experienced nature of technology surrounded even our fore-fathers and their things. Rilke's reflection is pertinent not be-cause it attempts still to salvage the things of our forefathers. Thinking ahead more fully, we must recognize what it is that becomes questionable along with the thingness of things. In-deed, still earlier—on March 1, 1912—Rilke writes from Duino: "The world draws into itself; for things, too, do the same in their turn, by shifting their existence more and more over into the vibrations of money, and developing there for themselves a kind of spirituality, which even now already sur-passes their palpable reality. In the age with which I am deal-ing" (Rilke is referring to the fourteenth century) "money was

---

* *Briefe aus Muzot*, pp. 335 f.

still gold, still metal, a beautiful thing, the handsomest, most comprehensible of all" (*Briefe,* 1907–1914, pp. 213 ff.). And still a decade earlier, in the *Book of Pilgrimage* (1901), second part of the *Book of Hours,* he published the highly prophetic lines:

> The kings of the world are grown old,
> inheritors they shall have none.
> In childhood death removes the son,
> their daughters pale have given, each one,
> sick crowns to the powers to hold.
>
> Into coin the rabble breaks them,
> today's lord of the world takes them,
> stretches them into machines in his fire,
> grumbling they serve his every desire;
> but happiness still forsakes them.
>
> The ore is homesick. And it yearns
> to leave the coin and leave the wheel
> that teach it to lead a life inane.
> The factories and tills it spurns;
> from petty forms it will uncongeal,
> return to the open mountain's vein,
> and on it the mountain will close again.*

In place of all the world-content of things that was formerly perceived and used to grant freely of itself, the object-character of technological dominion spreads itself over the earth ever more quickly, ruthlessly, and completely. Not only does it establish all things as producible in the process of production; it also delivers the products of production by means of the market. In self-assertive production, the humanness of man and the thing-

---

* *Gesammelte Werke,* II, 254. [Leipzig: Insel-Verlag, Volumes I–VI, 1927, Volumes VI–IX, 1930.—Tr.]

ness of things dissolve into the calculated market value of a market which not only spans the whole earth as a world market, but also, as the will to will, trades in the nature of Being and thus subjects all beings to the trade of a calculation that dominates most tenaciously in those areas where there is no need of numbers.

Rilke's poem thinks of man as the being who is ventured into a willing, the being who, without as yet experiencing it, is willed in the will to will. Willing in this way, man can go with the venture in such a way as to set himself up as the end and goal of everything. Thus man is more venturous than plant or beast. Accordingly, he also is in danger differently from them.

Among those beings, plants and beasts, too, none is under special protection, though they are admitted into the Open and secured in it. Man, on the other hand, as the being who wills himself, not only enjoys no special protection from the whole of beings, but rather is unshielded (line 13). As the one who proposes and produces, he stands before the obstructed Open. He himself and his things are thereby exposed to the growing danger of turning into mere material and into a function of objectification. The design of self-assertion itself extends the realm of the danger that man will lose his selfhood to unconditional production. The menace which assails man's nature arises from that nature itself. Yet human nature resides in the relation of Being to man, its draft upon him. Thus man, by his self-willing, becomes in an essential sense endangered, that is, in need of protection; but by that same nature he becomes at the same time unshielded.

This "our unshieldedness" (lines 12–13) remains different from the absence of special protection for plant and beast in the same measure as their "dim delight" differs from man's self-willing. The difference is infinite, because from the dim delight there is no transition to the objectification in self-assertion. But this self-assertion not only places man outside all care or protection; the imposition of the objectifying of the world destroys ever more resolutely the very possibility of protection. By building the world up technologically as an object, man deliberately and completely blocks his path, already obstructed, into the Open. Self-assertive man, whether or not he knows and wills it as an individual, is the functionary of technology. Not only does he face the Open from outside it; he even turns his back upon the "pure draft" by objectifying the world. Man sets himself apart from the pure draft. The man of the age of technology, by this parting, opposes himself to the Open. This parting is not a parting *from,* it is a parting *against.*

Technology is the unconditional establishment, posed by man's self-assertion, of unconditional unshieldedness on the ground of that turn which prevails in all objectiveness against the pure draft, by which the unheard-of center of beings draws all pure forces to itself. Technological production is the organization of this parting. The word for parting—*Abschied*—in the meaning just sketched, is another basic word in Rilke's valid poetry.

What is deadly is not the much-discussed atomic bomb as this particular death-dealing machine. What has long since been threatening man with death, and indeed with the death of his own nature, is the unconditional character of mere willing in the sense of purposeful self-assertion in everything. What threatens man in his very nature is the willed view that man, by the peaceful release, transformation, storage, and channeling of the energies of physical nature, could render the human condition, man's being, tolerable for everybody and happy in all respects. But the peace of this peacefulness is merely the undisturbed continuing relentlessness of the fury of self-assertion which is resolutely self-reliant. What threatens man in his very nature is the view that this imposition of production can be ventured without any danger, as long as other interests besides —such as, perhaps, the interests of a faith—retain their currency. As though it were still possible for that essential relation to the whole of beings in which man is placed by the technological exercise of his will to find a separate abode in some side-structure which would offer more than a temporary escape into those self-deceptions among which we must count also the flight to the Greek gods! What threatens man in his very nature is the view that technological production puts the world in order, while in fact this ordering is precisely what levels every *ordo,* every rank, down to the uniformity of production, and thus from the outset destroys the realm from which any rank and recognition could possibly arise.

It is not only the totality of this willing that is dangerous, but willing itself, in the form of self-assertion within a world that is admitted only as will. The willing that is willed by this will is already resolved to take unconditional command. By that resolve, it is even now delivered into the hands of total organization. But above all, technology itself prevents any experience of its nature. For while it is developing its own self to the full, it develops in the sciences a kind of knowing that is debarred from ever entering into the realm of the essential nature of technology, let alone retracing in thought that nature's origin.

The essence of technology comes to the light of day only slowly. This day is the world's night, rearranged into merely technological day. This day is the shortest day. It threatens a single endless winter. Not only does protection now withhold itself from man, but the integralness of the whole of what is remains now in darkness. The wholesome and sound withdraws. The world becomes without healing, unholy. Not only does the holy, as the track to the godhead, thereby remain concealed; even the track to the holy, the hale and whole, seems to be effaced. That is, unless there are still some mortals capable of seeing the threat of the unhealable, the unholy, *as* such. They would have to discern the danger that is assailing man. The danger consists in the threat that assaults man's nature in his relation to Being itself, and not in accidental perils. This danger is *the* danger. It conceals itself in the abyss that underlies all beings. To see this danger and point it out, there must be mortals who reach sooner into the abyss.

> But where there is danger, there grows
> also what saves.
>   Hölderlin, IV, 190*

It may be that any other salvation than that which comes from *where the* danger is, is still within the unholy. Any salvation by makeshift, however well-intentioned, remains for the duration of his destiny an insubstantial illusion for man, who is endangered in his nature. The salvation must come from where there is a turn with mortals in their nature. Are there mortals who reach sooner into the abyss of the destitute and its destituteness? These, the most mortal among mortals, would be the most daring, the most ventured. They would be still more daring even than that self-assertive human nature which is already more daring than plant and beast.

Rilke says in lines 6 ff.:

> Except that we, more eager than plant or beast,
> go *with* this venture, will it, ...

and then he continues, in the same lines:

> . . . adventurous
> more sometimes than Life itself is, more daring
> by a breath (and not in the least
> from selfishness) . . . .

Not only is man by nature more daring than plant and beast. Man is at times more daring even "than Life itself is." Life here means beings in their Being: Nature. Man is at times more venturesome than the venture, more fully (abundantly) being than the Being of beings. But Being is the ground of beings. He who is more venturesome than that ground ventures to

---

* Friedrich Hölderlin, *Sämtliche Werke,* edited by N. v. Hellingrath, F. Seebass, & L. v. Pigenot. 1st edition, Munich: 1913–1916. 2nd edition, 6 vols., Berlin: 1922–1923. 3rd edition, vols. 1–4, Berlin: 1943.—Tr.

where all ground breaks off—into the abyss. But if man is the ventured being who goes with the venture by willing it, then those men who are at times more venturesome must also will more strongly. Can there, however, be a heightening of this willing beyond the absolute of purposeful self-assertion? No. Those, then, who are at times more venturesome can will more strongly only if their willing is different in nature. Thus, willing and willing would not be the same right off. Those who will more strongly by the nature of willing, remain more in accord with the will as the Being of beings. They answer sooner to Being that shows itself as will. They will more strongly in that they are more willing. Who are these more willing ones who are more venturesome? To this question the poem, it seems, gives no explicit answer.

True, lines 8 to 11 say something about the more venturesome ones, negatively and by approximation. The more venturesome ones do not venture themselves out of selfishness, for their own personal sake. They seek neither to gain an advantage nor to indulge their self-interest. Nor, even though they are more venturesome, can they boast of any outstanding accomplishments. For they are more daring only by a little, "more daring by a breath." The "more" of their venture is as slight as a breath which remains fleeting and imperceptible. These hints do not allow us to gather who the more venturesome ones are.

Lines 10 and 11, however, tell what this daring brings which ventures beyond the Being of beings:

> There, outside all caring,
> this creates for us a safety—just there,
> where the pure forces' gravity rules. . . .

Like all beings, we are in being only by being ventured in the venture of Being. But because, as the beings who will, we go with the venture, we are more venturesome and thus sooner exposed to danger. When man entrenches himself in purposeful self-assertion, and by means of absolute objectification installs himself in the parting against the Open, then he himself promotes his own unshieldedness.

But the daring which is more venturesome creates a safety for us. It does not do so, to be sure, by raising protective defenses around the unprotected; in that way, a protection would be raised only in those places where protection is lacking. And that would once again require a production. Production is possible only in objectification. Objectification, however, blocks us off against the Open. The more venturesome daring does not produce a defense. But it creates a safety, a secureness for us. Secure, *securus, sine cura* means: without care. The caring here has the character of purposeful self-assertion by the ways and means of unconditional production. We are without such care only when we do not establish our nature exclusively within the precinct of production and procurement, of things that can be utilized and defended. We are secure only where we neither reckon with the unprotected nor count on a defense erected within willing. A safety exists only outside the objectifying turning away from the Open, "outside all caring," outside the parting against the pure draft. That draft is the unheard-of center of all attraction which draws all things into the boundless, and draws them for the center. This center is "there," where the gravity of the pure forces rules. To be secure is to repose safely within the drawing of the whole draft.

The daring that is more venturesome, willing more strongly than any self-assertion, because it is willing, "creates" a secureness for us in the Open. To create means to fetch from the source. And to fetch from the source means to take up what springs forth and to bring what has so been received. The more venturesome daring of the willing exercise of the will manufactures nothing. It receives, and gives what it has received. It brings, by unfolding in its fullness what it has received. The more venturesome daring accomplishes, but it does not produce. Only a daring that becomes more daring by being willing can accomplish in receiving.

Lines 12 to 16 circumscribe what the more venturesome daring consists in, which ventures itself outside all protection, and there brings us to a secureness. This safety does not at all remove that unshieldedness which is put there by purposeful self-assertion. When human nature is absorbed in the objectification of beings, it remains unprotected in the midst of beings. Unprotected in this way, man remains related to protection, in the mode of lacking it, and thereby he remains within protection. Secureness, on the contrary, is outside all relation to protection, "outside all caring."

Accordingly, it seems that secureness, and our reaching secureness, call for a daring that surrenders all relation to being shielded and unshielded. But it only seems that way. The truth is that when our thinking proceeds from the enclosure of the whole draft, we then finally experience that which in the end— that is, beforehand—relieves us of the care of unprotected self- imposition (lines 12 ff.):

> . . . in the end,
> it is our unshieldedness on which we depend. . . .

How is unshieldedness supposed to keep us safe, when only the Open affords safety, while unshieldedness consists in the constant parting against the Open? Unshieldedness can keep us safe only when the parting against the Open is inverted, so that it turns toward the Open—and into it. Thus, what keeps safe is unshieldedness in reverse. Keeping means here, for one thing, that the inversion of the parting performs the safekeeping, and for another, that unshieldedness itself, in a certain manner, grants a safety. What keeps us safe is

> . . . our unshieldedness . . .
> and that, when we saw it threatening, we turned it
> so into the Open. . . .

The "and" leads over into the explanation which tells in what manner this strange thing is possible, that our unshieldedness, outside all protection, grants us a safety. Unshieldedness will, of course, never safeguard us if we invert it only from case to case, whenever it threatens. Unshieldedness keeps safe only if we have already turned it. Rilke says: "that . . . we turned it/ so into the Open . . . ." In our having turned it there is implied a distinctive manner of conversion. In our having turned it, unshieldedness is turned from the outset, as a whole, in its nature. The distinctive feature of the conversion consists in our having seen unshieldedness as what is threatening us. Only such a having-seen sees the danger. It sees that unshieldedness as such threatens our nature with the loss of our belonging to the Open. The conversion must lie in this having-seen. It is then that unshieldedness is turned "into the Open." By having seen the danger as the threat to our human being, we must have accomplished the inversion of the parting against the Open. This implies: the Open itself must have turned toward us in a way that allows us to turn our unshieldedness toward it,

> so into the Open that, in widest orbit somewhere,
> where the Law touches us, we may affirm it.

What is the widest orbit? Presumably Rilke is thinking of the Open, and indeed in a specific respect. The widest orbit surrounds all that is. The orbiting rounds into one all beings, so that, in the unifying, it is the Being of beings. But what does "being" mean? The poet, to be sure, designates beings as a whole with the names "Nature," "Life," "the Open," "the whole draft." Following the habits of the language of metaphysics, he even calls this rounded whole of beings "Being." But we do not learn what the nature of Being is. And yet, does not Rilke speak of it when he calls Being the venture that ventures all? Certainly. Accordingly, we tried to trace in thought what has been so designated back to the modern nature of the Being of beings, the will to will. And yet, what is said about the widest orbit does not tell us anything definite when we try to think of what was mentioned as the whole of beings, and of the orbiting as the Being of beings.

As thinking beings we think back, of course, to the fact that the Being of beings has from the beginning been thought of with regard to the orbiting. But we think of this spherical aspect of Being too loosely, and always only on the surface, unless we have already asked and learned how the Being of beings occurs initially. The *eon,* being, of the *eonta,* beings as a whole, is called the *hen,* the unifying One. But what is this encircling unifying as a fundamental trait of being? What does Being mean? *Eon,* "in being," signifies present, and indeed present in the unconcealed. But in presence there is concealed the bringing on of unconcealedness which lets the present beings occur as such. But only Presence itself is truly present—Presence which is everywhere as the Same in its own center and, as such, is the sphere. The spherical does not consist in a circuit which then embraces, but in the unconcealing center that, lightening, safeguards present beings. The sphericity of the unifying, and the unifying itself, have the character of unconcealing lightening, within which present beings can be present. This is why Parmenides (Fragment VIII, 42) calls the *eon,* the presence of what is present, the *eukuklos sphaire.* This well-rounded sphere is to be thought of as the Being of beings, in the sense of the unconcealing-lightening unifying. This unifier, uniting everywhere in this manner, prompts us to call it the lightening shell, which precisely does not embrace since it uncovers and reveals, but which itself releases, lightening, into Presence. We must never represent this sphere of Being and its sphericity as an object. Must we then present it as a nonobject? No; that would be a mere flight to a manner of speaking. The spherical must be thought by way of the nature of primal Being in the sense of unconcealing Presence.

Rilke's words about the widest orbit—do they mean this sphericity of Being? Not only does nothing allow us to think so, but what is more, the characterization of the Being of beings as venture (will) argues positively against it. Yet Rilke himself, on one occasion, speaks of the "globe of being," and does so in a context which touches directly on the interpretation of the statement about the widest orbit. In a letter of January 6, 1923 (see *Insel-Almanach* 1938,* p. 109), Rilke writes:

". . . like the moon, so life surely has a side that is constantly turned away from us, and that is not its opposite but its completion to perfection, to plenitude, to the real, whole, and full sphere and globe of being." Though we must not press the figurative reference to the celestial body represented as an object, it nevertheless remains clear that Rilke is here thinking of sphericity not in regard to Being in the sense of lightening-unifying Presence, but in regard to beings in the sense of the plenitude of all their facets. The globe of Being of which he speaks here, that is, the globe of all beings as a whole, is the Open, as the pure forces serried, boundlessly flowing into one another and thus acting toward one another. The widest orbit is the wholeness of the whole draft of attraction. To this widest circle there corresponds as the strongest center, the "unheard-of center" of pure gravity.

To turn unshieldedness into the Open means to "affirm" unshieldedness within the widest orbit. Such a yea-saying is possible only where the whole of the orbit is in every respect not only in full measure, but commensurate, and is already before us as such and, accordingly, is the *positum*. Only a positing can correspond to it, never a negating. Even those sides of life that are averted from us must, insofar as they are, be taken positively. In the letter of November 13, 1925 already mentioned, we read: "Death is the *side of life* that is averted from us, unillumined by us" (*Briefe aus Muzot*, p. 332). Death and the realm of the dead belong to the whole of beings as its other side. That realm is "the other draft," that is, the other side of the whole draft of the Open. Within the widest orbit of the

* [Leipzig: Insel-Verlag.—Tr.]

sphere of beings there are regions and places which, being averted from us, seem to be something negative, but are nothing of the kind if we think of all things as being within the widest orbit of beings.

Seen from the Open, unshieldedness too, as the parting against the pure draft, seems to be something negative. The parting self-assertion of objectification wills everywhere the constancy of produced objects, and recognizes it alone as being and as positive. The self-assertion of technological objectification is the constant negation of death. By this negation death itself becomes something negative; it becomes the altogether inconstant and null. But if we turn unshieldedness into the Open, we turn it into the widest orbit of beings, within which we can only affirm unshieldedness. To turn it into the Open is to renounce giving a negative reading to that which is. But what is more in being—in terms of modern thought, what is more certain—than death? The letter of January 6, 1923, cited earlier, says that the point is "to read the word 'death' *without* negation."

If we turn unshieldedness as such into the Open, we then convert its nature—that is, as the parting against the whole draft—into a turning toward the widest orbit. Nothing is then left for us but to affirm what has been so converted. This affirmation, however, does not mean to turn a No into a Yes; it means to acknowledge the positive as what is already before us and present. We do so by allowing the converted unshieldedness within the widest orbit to belong "where the Law touches us." Rilke does not say "a law." Nor does he mean a rule. He is thinking of what "touches us." Who are we? We are those who will, who set up the world as object by way of intentional self-assertion. When we are touched from out of the widest orbit, the touch goes to our very nature, To touch means to touch off, to set in motion. Our nature is set in motion. The will is shaken by the touch so that only now is the nature of willing made to appear and set in motion. Not until then do we will willingly.

But what is it that touches us directly out of the widest orbit? What is it that remains blocked off, withdrawn from us by ourselves in our ordinary willing to objectify the world? It is the other draft: Death. Death is what touches mortals in their nature, and so sets them on their way to the other side of life, and so into the whole of the pure draft. Death thus gathers into the whole of what is already posited, into the *positum* of the whole draft. As this gathering of positing, death is the laying-down, the Law, just as the mountain chain is the gathering of the mountains into the whole of its chain. There, where the Law touches us, there is the place within the widest orbit into which we can admit the converted unshieldedness positively into the whole of what is. Our unshieldedness, so converted, finally shelters us within the Open, outside all protection. But how is the turning possible? In what way can the conversion of the parting against the Open come about? Presumably only in this way, that the conversion first turns us toward the widest orbit, and prompts us, ourselves, in our nature, to turn toward and into it. The region of secureness must first be shown to us, it must be accessible beforehand as the possible arena of conversion. But what brings us a secure being, and with it generally the dimension of security, is that daring venture which is at times more daring even than Life itself.

But this more daring venture does not tinker here and there with our unshieldedness. It does not attempt to change this or that way of objectifying the world. Rather, it turns unshieldedness as such. The more daring venture carries unshieldedness precisely into the realm that is its own.

What is the nature of unshieldedness, if it consists in that objectification which lies in purposeful self-assertion? What stands as object in the world becomes *standing* in representational production. Such representation presents. But what is present is present in a representation that has the character of calculation. Such representation knows nothing immediately perceptual. What can be immediately seen when we look at things, the image they offer to immediate sensible intuition, falls away. The calculating production of technology is an "act without an image" (ninth of the *Duino Elegies,* line 46). Purposeful self-assertion, with its designs, interposes before the intuitive image the project of the merely calculated product. When the world enters into the objectness of the thought-devised product, it is placed within the nonsensible, the invisible. What stands thus owes its presence to a placing whose activity belongs to the *res cogitans,* that is, to consciousness. The sphere of the objectivity of objects remains inside consciousness. What is invisible in that which stands-over-against belongs to the interior and immanence of consciousness.

But if unshieldedness is the parting against the Open, while yet the parting lies in the objectification that belongs to the invisible and interior of calculating consciousness, then the natural sphere of unshieldedness is the invisible and interior of consciousness.

But since the turning of unshieldedness into the Open concerns the nature of unshieldedness from the very start, this conversion of unshieldedness is a conversion of consciousness, and that *inside* the sphere of consciousness. The sphere of the invisible and interior determines the nature of unshieldedness, but also the manner in which it is turned into the widest orbit. Thus, that toward which the essentially inner and invisible must turn to find its own can itself only be the most invisible of the invisible and the innermost of the inner. In modern metaphysics, the sphere of the invisible interior is defined as the realm of the presence of calculated objects. Descartes describes this sphere as the consciousness of the *ego cogito.*

At nearly the same time as Descartes, Pascal discovers the logic of the heart as over against the logic of calculating reason. The inner and invisible domain of the heart is not only more inward than the interior that belongs to calculating representation, and therefore more invisible; it also extends further than does the realm of merely producible objects. Only in the invisible innermost of the heart is man inclined toward what there is for him to love: the forefathers, the dead, the children, those who are to come. All this belongs in the widest orbit, which now proves to be the sphere of the presence of the whole integral draft. True, this presence too, like that of the customary consciousness of calculating production, is a presence of immanence. But the interior of uncustomary consciousness remains the inner space in which everything is for us beyond the arithmetic of calculation, and, free of such boundaries, can overflow into the unbounded whole of the Open. This overflow beyond number rises, in its presence, in the inner and invisible region of the heart. The last lines of the ninth elegy, which sings man's belonging to the Open, run: "Existence beyond number/wells up in my heart."

The widest orbit of beings becomes present in the heart's inner space. The whole of the world achieves here an equally essential presence in all its drawings. Rilke, in the language of metaphysics, here speaks of "existence." The world's whole presence is in the widest sense "worldly existence." That is another name for the Open, other because of the different manner of naming, which now thinks the Open, insofar as the representing-producing parting against the Open has now reversed itself, from the immanence of calculating consciousness toward the inner space of the heart. The heart's inner space for worldly existence is therefore also called the "world's inner realm." "Worldly" means the whole of all beings.

In a letter from Muzot dated August 11, 1924, Rilke writes:

However vast the "outer space" may be, yet with all its sidereal distances it hardly bears comparison with the dimensions, *with the depth dimensions of our inner being,* which does not even need the spaciousness of the universe to be within itself almost unfathomable. Thus, if the dead, if those who are to come, need an abode, *what* refuge could be more agreeable and appointed for them than this imaginary space? To me it seems more and more as though our customary consciousness lives on the tip of a pyramid whose base within us (and in a certain way beneath us) widens out so fully that the farther we find ourselves able to descend into it, the more generally we appear to be merged into those things that, independent of time and space, are given in our earthly, in the widest sense worldly, existence.

By contrast, the objectness of the world remains reckoned in that manner of representation which deals with time and space as *quanta* of calculation, and which can know no more of the nature of time than of the nature of space. Rilke, too, gives no further thought to the spatiality of the world's inner space; even less does he ask whether the world's inner space, giving its abode to worldly presence, is by this presence grounded in a temporality whose essential time, together with essential space, forms the original unity of that time-space by which even Being itself presences.

Rilke attempts, however, within the spherical structure of modern metaphysics, that is, within the sphere of subjectivity as the sphere of inner and invisible presence, to understand the unshieldedness established by man's self-assertive nature, in such a way that this unshieldedness itself, having been turned about, safeguards us in the innermost and most invisible region of the widest inner space of the world. Unshieldedness safeguards as such. For it gives to man's nature, as inward and invisible, the clue for a conversion of the parting against the Open. The conversion points to the innermost region of the interior. The conversion of consciousness, therefore, is an inner recalling of the immanence of the objects of representation into presence within the heart's space.

As long as man is wholly absorbed in nothing but purposeful self-assertion, not only is he himself unshielded, but so are things, because they have become objects. In this, to be sure, there also lies a transmutation of things into what is inward and invisible. But this transmutation replaces the frailties of things by the thought-contrived fabrications of calculated objects. These objects are produced to be used up. The more quickly they are used up, the greater becomes the necessity to replace them even more quickly and more readily. What is lasting in the presence of objective things is not their self-subsistence within the world that is their own. What is constant in things produced as objects merely for consumption is: the substitute—*Ersatz*.

Just as it is a part of our unshieldedness that the familiar things fade away under the predominance of objectness, so also our nature's safety demands the rescue of things from mere objectness. The rescue consists in this, that things, within the widest orbit of the whole draft, can be at rest within themselves, which means that they can rest without restriction within one another. Indeed, it may well be that the turning of our unshieldedness into worldly existence within the world's inner space must begin with this, that we turn the transient and therefore preliminary character of object-things away from the inner and invisible region of the merely producing consciousness and toward the true interior of the heart's space, and there allow it to arise invisibly. Accordingly the letter of November 13, 1925 (*Briefe aus Muzot,* p. 335) says:

". . . our task is to impress this preliminary, transient earth upon ourselves with so much suffering and so passionately that its nature rises up again 'invisibly' within us. *We are the bees of the invisible.* Nous butinons éperdument le miel du visible, pour l'accumuler dans la grande ruche d'or de l'Invisible." (We ceaselessly gather the honey of the visible, to store it up in the great golden beehive of the Invisible.)

The inner recalling converts that nature of ours which merely wills to impose, together with its objects, into the innermost invisible region of the heart's space. Here everything is inward: not only does it remain turned toward this true interior of consciousness, but inside this interior, one thing turns, free of all bounds, into the other. The interiority of the world's inner space unbars the Open for us. Only what we thus retain in our heart (*par coeur*), only that do we truly know by heart. Within this interior we are free, outside of the relation to the objects set around us that only seem to give protection. In the interiority of the world's inner space there is a safety outside all shielding.

But, we have been asking all along, how can this inner re-calling of the already immanent objectness of consciousness into the heart's innermost region come about? It concerns the inner and invisible. For that which is inwardly recalled, as well as the place to which it is recalled, is of such a nature. The inner recalling is the conversion of the parting into an arriving at the widest orbit of the Open. Who among mortals is capable of this converting recall?

To be sure, the poem says that a secureness of our nature comes to us by man's being

> . . . adventurous
> more sometimes than Life itself is, more daring
> by a breath . . . .

What do they dare, those who are more daring? The poem, it seems, withholds the answer. We shall therefore try to meet the poem halfway in thought, and we shall also draw on other poems for help.

We ask: what is there still to be dared that would be still more daring than Life, which is itself the daring venture, so that it would be more daring than the Being of beings? In every case and in every respect, what is dared must be such that it concerns every being inasmuch as it is a being. Of such a kind is Being, and in this way, that it is not one particular kind among others, but the mode of all beings as such.

If Being is what is unique to beings, by what can Being still be surpassed? Only by itself, only by its own, and indeed by expressly entering into its own. Then Being would be the unique which wholly surpasses itself (the *transcendens* pure and simple). But this surpassing, this transcending does not go up and over into something else; it comes up to its own self and back into the nature of its truth. Being itself traverses this going over and is itself its dimension.

When we think on this, we experience within Being itself that there lies in it something "more" belonging to it, and thus the possibility that there too, where Being is thought of as the venture, something more daring may prevail than even Being itself, so far as we commonly conceive Being in terms of particular beings. Being, as itself, spans its own province, which is marked off (*temnein, tempus*) by Being's being present in the word. Language is the precinct (*templum*), that is, the house of Being. The nature of language does not exhaust itself in signifying, nor is it merely something that has the character of sign or cipher. It is because language is the house of Being, that we reach what is by constantly going through this house. When we go to the well, when we go through the woods, we are always already going through the word "well," through the word "woods," even if we do not speak the words and do not think of anything relating to language. Thinking our way from the temple of Being, we have an intimation of what they dare who are sometimes more daring than the Being of beings. They dare the precinct of Being. They dare language. All beings—objects of consciousness and things of the heart, men who impose themselves and men who are more daring—all beings, each in its own way, are *qua* beings in the precinct of language. This is why the return from the realm of objects and their representation into the innermost region of the heart's space can be accomplished, if anywhere, *only in this precinct.*

For Rilke's poetry, the Being of beings is metaphysically defined as worldly presence; this presence remains referred to representation in consciousness, whether that consciousness has the character of the immanence of calculating representation, or that of the inward conversion to the Open which is accessible through the heart.

The whole sphere of presence is present in saying. The objectness, the standing-over-against, of production stands in the assertion of calculating propositions and of the theorems of the reason that proceeds from proposition to proposition. The realm of self-assertive unshieldedness is dominated by reason. Not only has reason established a special system of rules for its saying, for the *logos* as declarative prediction; the logic of reason is itself the organization of the dominion of purposeful self-assertion in the objective. In the conversion of objective representation, the logic of the heart corresponds to the saying of the inner recall. In both realms, which are determined metaphysically, logic prevails, because the inner recalling is supposed to create a secureness, out of unshieldedness itself and outside all shielding. This safekeeping is of concern to man as the being who has language. He has language within the Being that bears the stamp of metaphysics, in this way, that he takes language from the start and merely as something he has in hand, like a personal belonging, and thus as a handle for his representation and conduct. This is why the *logos,* saying *qua* organon, requires organization by logic. Only within metaphysics does logic exist.

But when, in the creation of a safety, man is touched by the Law of the world's whole inner space, he is himself touched in his nature, in that, as the being who wills himself, he is already the sayer. But since the creation of a safety comes from the more venturesome, these more venturesome ones must dare the venture with language. The more venturesome dare the saying. But if the precinct of this daring, language, belongs to Being in that unique manner above which and beyond which there can be nothing else of its kind, in what direction is that to be said which the sayers must say? Their saying concerns the inner recalling conversion of consciousness which turns our unshieldedness into the invisible of the world's inner space. Their saying, because it concerns the conversion, speaks not only from both realms but from the oneness of the two, insofar as that oneness has already come to be as the saving unification. Therefore, where the whole of all beings is thought of as the Open of the pure draft, the inner recalling conversion must be a saying which says what it has to say to a being who is already secure in the whole of all beings, because he has already accomplished the transmutation of what is visible in representation into that which is an invisible of the heart. This being is drawn into the pure draft by one side and the other of the globe of Being. This being, for whom borderlines and differences between the drawings hardly exist any longer, is the being who governs the unheard-of center of the widest orbit and causes it to appear. This being, in Rilke's *Duino Elegies,* is the Angel. This name is once again a basic word in Rilke's poetry. Like "the Open," "the draft," "the parting," "Nature," it is a basic word because what is said in it thinks the whole of beings by way of Being. In his letter of November 13, 1925 Rilke writes:

"The Angel of the *Elegies* is that creature in whom the transmutation of the visible into the invisible, which we achieve, seems already accomplished. The Angel of the *Elegies* is that being who assures the recognition of a higher order of reality in the invisible."*

Only a more primal elucidation of the nature of subjectness will serve to show how, within the completion of modern metaphysics, there belongs to the Being of beings a relation to such a being, how the creature which is Rilke's Angel, despite all difference in content, is *metaphysically the same* as the figure of Nietzsche's Zarathustra.

The poem thinks of the Being of beings, Nature, as the venture. Every being is ventured in a venture. As ventured, it now lies in the balance. The balance is the way in which Being ever and again weighs beings, that is, keeps them in the motion of weighing. Everything ventured is in danger. The realms of beings may be distinguished by the kind of relation they have to the balance. The nature of the Angel, too, must become clearer with respect to the balance, assuming he is of higher rank in the whole realm of beings.

Plant and beast, "in the venture of their dim delight," are held carefree in the Open. Their bodily character does not perplex them. By their drives, the living creatures are lulled into

---

* *Briefe aus Muzot,* p. 337.

the Open. They too remain in danger, to be sure, but not in their nature. Plant and beast lie in the balance in such a way that the balance always settles into the repose of a secureness. The balance in which plant and beast are ventured does not yet reach into the realm of what is in essence and thus constantly unstilled. The balance in which the Angel is ventured also remains outside of what is unstilled—not, however, because it does not yet belong to the realm of the unstilled, but because it belongs there no longer. In keeping with his bodiless nature, possible confusion by what is sensibly visible has been transmuted into the invisible. The Angel is in being by virtue of the stilled repose of the balanced oneness of the two realms within the world's inner space.

Man, on the contrary, as the one who purposely asserts himself, is ventured into unshieldedness. In the hands of man who has been so ventured, the balance of danger is in essence unstilled. Self-willing man everywhere reckons with things and men as with objects. What is so reckoned becomes merchandise. Everything is constantly changed about into new orders. The parting against the pure draft establishes itself within the unstilled agitation of the constantly balancing balance. By its objectification of the world, the parting, contrary to its own intention, promotes inconstancy. Thus ventured into the unshielded, man moves within the medium of "businesses" and "exchanges." Self-assertive man lives by staking his will. He lives essentially by risking his nature in the vibration of money and the currency of values. As this constant trader and middleman, man is the "merchant." He weighs and measures constantly, yet does not know the real weight of things. Nor does he ever know what in himself is truly weighty and preponderant. In one of his late poems (*Späte Gedichte,* p. 21 f.) Rilke says:

> Alas, who knows what in himself prevails.
> Mildness? Terror? Glances, voices, books?

But at the same time, man who is outside all protection can procure a safety by turning unshieldedness as such into the Open and transmuting it into the heart's space of the invisible. If that happens, then what is unstilled in unshieldedness passes over to where, in the balanced oneness of the world's inner space, there appears the being who brings out the radiant appearance of the way in which that oneness unifies, and who in this way represents Being. The balance of danger then passes out of the realm of calculating will over to the Angel. Four lines have been preserved from Rilke's late period which apparently constitute the beginning of a sketch for a larger poem (*Gesammelte Werke,* III, 438). For the present, no further word about them is needed. They run:

> . . . When from the merchant's hand
> the balance passes over
> to that Angel who, in the heavens,
> stills it, appeases it by the equalizing of space . . . .

The equalizing space is the world's inner space, in that it gives space to the worldly whole of the Open. Thus the space grants to the one and to the other draft the appearance of their unifying oneness. That oneness, as the integral globe of Being, encircles all pure forces of what is, by circling through all beings, in-finitely unbounding them. All this becomes present when the balance passes over. When does it pass over? Who makes the balance pass over from the merchant to the Angel? If such a passing comes to pass at all, it occurs in the precinct of the balance. The element of the balance is the venture, the Being of beings. We have thought of language specifically as its precinct.

The customary life of contemporary man is the common life of the imposition of self on the unprotected market of the exchangers. By contrast, the passage of the balance to the Angel is uncommon. It is uncommon even in the sense that it not only constitutes the exception to the rule, but that it takes man, in respect of his nature, outside and beyond the rule of protection and unprotectedness. This is why the passing-on occurs "sometimes." "Sometimes" here does not at all mean occasionally and at random. "Sometimes" signifies: rarely and at the right time in an always unique instance in a unique manner. The passing over of the balance from the merchant to the Angel, that is, the conversion of the parting, occurs as the inner recalling into the world's inner space at that time when there are men who are

> . . . adventurous
> more sometimes than Life itself is, more daring
> by a breath. . . .

Because these more venturesome ones venture Being itself and therefore dare to venture into language, the province of Being, they are the sayers. And yet, is not man the one who by his nature has language and constantly ventures it? Certainly. And then even he who wills in the usual way ventures saying, already in calculating production. True. But then, those who are more venturesome cannot be those who merely say. The saying of the more venturesome must really venture to *say*. The more venturesome are the ones they are only when they are sayers to a greater degree.

When, in relation to beings in terms of representation and production, we relate ourselves at the same time by making propositional assertions, such a saying is not what is willed. Asserting remains a way and a means. By contrast, there is a saying that really engages in saying, yet without reflecting upon language, which would make even language into one more object. To be involved in saying is the mark of a saying that follows something to be said, solely in order to say it. What is to be said would then be what by nature belongs to the province of language. And that, thought metaphysically, is particular beings as a whole. Their wholeness is the intactness of the pure draft, the sound wholeness of the Open, in that it makes room within itself for man. This happens in the world's inner space. That space touches man when, in the inner recalling of conversion, he turns toward the space of the heart. The more venturesome ones turn the unwholesomeness of unshieldedness into the soundness of worldly existence. This is what is to be said. In the saying it turns itself toward man. The more venturesome are those who say in a greater degree, in the manner of the singer. Their singing is turned away from all purposeful self-assertion. It is not a willing in the sense of desire. Their song does not solicit anything to be produced. In the song, the world's inner space concedes space within itself. The song of these singers is neither solicitation nor trade.

The saying of the more venturesome which is more fully saying is the song. But

Song is existence,

says the third of the *Sonnets to Orpheus,* Part I. The word for existence, *Dasein,* is used here in the traditional sense of presence and as a synonym of Being. To sing, truly to say worldly existence, to say out of the haleness of the whole pure draft and to say only this, means: to belong to the precinct of beings themselves. This precinct, as the very nature of language, is Being itself. To sing the song means to be present in what is present itself. It means: *Dasein,* existence.

But the saying that is more fully saying happens only sometimes, because only the more venturesome are capable of it. For it is still hard. The hard thing is to accomplish existence. The hard thing consists not only in the difficulty of forming the work of language, but in the difficulty of going over from the saying work of the still covetous vision of things, from the work of the eyes, to the "work of the heart." The song is hard because the singing may no longer be a solicitation, but must be existence. For the god Orpheus, who lives in-finitely in the Open, song is an easy matter, but not for man. This is why the final stanza of the sonnet referred to asks:

> But when *are* we?

The stress is on the "are," not on the "we." There is no question that we belong to what is, and that we are present in this respect. But it remains questionable when we are in such a way that our being is song, and indeed a song whose singing does not resound just anywhere but is truly a singing, a song whose sound does not cling to something that is eventually attained, but which has already shattered itself even in the sounding, so that there may occur only that which was sung itself. Men say more sayingly in this form when they are more venturesome than all that is, itself. These more venturesome ones are, according to the poem, "more daring by a breath." The sonnet from which we have quoted ends:

> To sing in truth is another breath.
> A breath for nothing. An afflatus in the god. A wind.

In his *Ideas on the Philosophy of the History of Man,* Herder writes as follows: "A breath of our mouth becomes the portrait of the world, the type of our thoughts and feelings in the other's soul. On a bit of moving air depends everything human that men on earth have ever thought, willed, done, and ever will do; for we would all still be roaming the forests if this divine breath had not blown around us, and did not hover on our lips like a magic tone" (W. W. Suphan XIII,* 140 f.).

The breath by which the more venturesome are more daring does not mean only or first of all the barely noticeable, because

---

* [Herder, Johann Gottfried. *Herders Sämmtliche Werke.* Edited by Bernhard Suphan, Carl Redlich, Reinhold Steig, *et al.* Berlin: Weidmannsche Buchhandlung, 1877–1913. 33 Vols.—Tr.]

evanescent, measure of a difference; rather, it means directly the word and the nature of language. Those who are more daring by a breath dare the venture with language. They are the sayers who more sayingly say. For this one breath by which they are more daring is not just a saying of any sort; rather, this one breath is another breath, a saying other than the rest of human saying. The other breath is no longer solicitous for this or that objective thing; it is a breath for nothing. The singer's saying says the sound whole of worldly existence, which invisibly offers its space within the world's inner space of the heart. The song does not even first follow what is to be said. The song is the belonging to the whole of the pure draft. Singing is drawn by the draft of the wind of the unheard-of center of full Nature. The song itself is "a wind."

Thus our poem does after all state unequivocally in poetic terms who they are that are more daring even than Life itself. They are those who are "more daring by a breath." It is not for nothing that the words "more daring by a breath" are followed in the original by three dots. The dots tell what is kept silent.

The more venturesome are the poets, but poets whose song turns our unprotected being into the Open. Because they convert the parting against the Open and inwardly recall its unwholesomeness into a sound whole, these poets sing the healing whole in the midst of the unholy. The recalling conversion has already overtaken the parting against the Open. It is "ahead of all parting" and outlives everything objective within the world's inner space of the heart. The converting inner recalling is the daring that dares to venture forth from the nature of man, because man has language and is he who says.

Modern man, however, is called the one who wills. The more venturesome will more strongly in that they will in a different way from the purposeful self-assertion of the objectifying of the world. Their willing wills nothing of this kind. If willing remains mere self-assertion, they will nothing. They will nothing, in this sense, because they are more willing. They answer sooner to the will which, as the venture itself, draws all pure forces to itself as the pure whole draft of the Open. The willing of the more venturesome is the willingness of those who say more sayingly, those who are resolved, no longer closed off in the parting against the will as which Being wills beings. The willing nature of the more venturesome says more sayingly (in the words of the ninth of the *Duino Elegies*):

> Earth, your will, is it not this: to rise up
> in us invisible? Is it not your dream
> one day to be invisible? Earth! invisible!
> What, if not transfiguration, is your pressing mission?
> Earth, dear one, I shall!

In the invisible of the world's inner space, as whose worldly oneness the Angel appears, the haleness of worldly beings becomes visible. Holiness can appear only within the widest orbit of the wholesome. Poets who are of the more venturesome kind are under way on the track of the holy because they experience the unholy as such. Their song over the land hallows. Their singing hails the integrity of the globe of Being.

The unholy, as unholy, traces the sound for us. What is sound beckons to the holy, calling it. The holy binds the divine. The divine draws the god near.

The more venturesome experience unshieldedness in the unholy. They bring to mortals the trace of the fugitive gods, the track into the dark of the world's night. As the singers of soundness, the more venturesome ones are "poets in a destitute time."

The mark of these poets is that to them the nature of poetry becomes worthy of questioning, because they are poetically on the track of that which, for them, is what must be said. On the track toward the wholesome, Rilke arrives at the poet's question: when is there song that sings essentially? This question does not stand at the beginning of the poet's way, but at the point where Rilke's saying attains to the poetic vocation of the kind of poet who answers to the coming world era. This era is neither a decay nor a downfall. As destiny, it lies in Being and lays claim to man.

Hölderlin is the pre-cursor of poets in a destitute time. This is why no poet of this world era can overtake him. The precursor, however, does not go off into a future; rather, he arrives out of that future, in such a way that the future is present only in the arrival of his words. The more purely the arrival happens, the more its remaining occurs as present. The greater the concealment with which what is to come maintains its reserve in the foretelling saying, the purer is the arrival. It would thus be mistaken to believe that Hölderlin's time will come only on that day when "everyman" will understand his poetry. It will never arrive in such a misshapen way; for it is its own destitution that endows the era with forces by which, unaware of what it is doing, it keeps Hölderlin's poetry from becoming timely.

If the precursor cannot be overtaken, no more can he perish; for his poetry remains as a once-present being. What occurs in the arrival gathers itself back into destiny. That which this way never lapses into the flux of perishing, overcomes from the start all perishability. What has merely passed away is without destiny even before it has passed. The once-present being, on the contrary, partakes in destiny. What is presumed to be eternal merely conceals a suspended transiency, suspended in the void of a durationless now.

If Rilke is a "poet in a destitute time" then only his poetry answers the question to what end he is a poet, whither his song is bound, where the poet belongs in the destiny of the world's night. That destiny decides what remains fateful within this poetry.

BUILDING   DWELLING   THINKING

BUILDING DWELLING THINKING

In what follows we shall try to think about dwelling and building. This thinking about building does not presume to discover architectural ideas, let alone to give rules for building. This venture in thought does not view building as an art or as a technique of construction; rather it traces building back into that domain to which everything that *is* belongs. We ask:

1. What is it to dwell?
2. How does building belong to dwelling?

I

We attain to dwelling, so it seems, only by means of building. The latter, building, has the former, dwelling, as its goal. Still, not every building is a dwelling. Bridges and hangars, stadiums and power stations are buildings but not dwellings; railway stations and highways, dams and market halls are built, but they are not dwelling places. Even so, these buildings are in the domain of our dwelling. That domain extends over these buildings and yet is not limited to the dwelling place. The truck driver is at home on the highway, but he does not have his shelter there; the working woman is at home in the spinning mill, but does not have her dwelling place there; the chief engineer is at home in the power station, but he does not dwell there. These buildings house man. He inhabits them and yet does not dwell in them, when to dwell means merely that we take shelter in them. In today's housing shortage even this much is reassuring and to the good; residential buildings do indeed provide shelter; today's houses may even be well planned, easy to keep, attractively cheap, open to air, light, and sun, but—do the houses in themselves hold any guarantee that *dwelling* occurs in them? Yet those buildings that are not dwelling places remain in turn determined by dwelling insofar as they serve man's dwelling. Thus dwelling would in any case be the end that presides over all building. Dwelling and building are related as end and means. However, as long as this is all we have in mind, we take dwelling and building as two separate activities, an idea that has something correct in it. Yet at the same time by the means-end schema we block our view of the essential relations. For building is not merely a means and a way toward dwelling —to build is in itself already to dwell. Who tells us this? Who gives us a standard at all by which we can take the measure of the nature of dwelling and building?

It is language that tells us about the nature of a thing, provided that we respect language's own nature. In the meantime, to be sure, there rages round the earth an unbridled yet clever talking, writing, and broadcasting of spoken words. Man acts as though *he* were the shaper and master of language, while in fact *language* remains the master of man. Perhaps it is before all else man's subversion of *this* relation of dominance that drives his nature into alienation. That we retain a concern for care in speaking is all to the good, but it is of no help to us as long as language still serves us even then only as a means of expression. Among all the appeals that we human beings, on our part, can help to be voiced, language is the highest and everywhere the first.

What, then, does *Bauen,* building, *mean?* The Old English and High German word for building, *buan,* means to dwell. This signifies: to remain, to stay in a place. The real meaning of the verb *bauen,* namely, to dwell, has been lost to us. But a covert trace of it has been preserved in the German word *Nachbar,* neighbor. The neighbor is in Old English the *neahgebur;*

neah, near, and *gebur,* dweller. The Nachbar is the *Nachgebur,* the *Nachgebauer,* the near-dweller, he who dwells nearby. The verbs *buri, büren, beuren, beuron,* all signify dwelling, the abode, the place of dwelling. Now to be sure the old word *buan* not only tells us that *bauen,* to build, is really to dwell; it also gives us a clue as to how we have to think about the dwelling it signifies. When we speak of dwelling we usually think of an activity that man performs alongside many other activities. We work here and dwell there. We do not merely dwell—that would be virtual inactivity—we practice a profession, we do business, we travel and lodge on the way, now here, now there. *Bauen* originally means to dwell. Where the word *bauen* still speaks in its original sense it also says *how far* the nature of dwelling reaches. That is, *bauen, buan, bhu, beo* are our word *bin* in the versions: *ich bin,* I am, *du bist,* you are, the imperative form *bis,* be. What then does *ich bin* mean? The old word *bauen,* to which the *bin* belongs, answers: *ich bin, du bist* mean: I dwell, you dwell. The way in which you are and I am, the manner in which we humans *are* on the earth, is *Buan,* dwelling. To be a human being means to be on the earth as a mortal. It means to dwell. The old word *bauen,* which says that man *is* insofar as he *dwells,* this word *bauen* however *also* means at the same time to cherish and protect, to preserve and care for, specifically to till the soil, to cultivate the vine. Such building only takes care—it tends the growth that ripens into its fruit of its own accord. Building in the sense of preserving and nurturing is not making anything. Shipbuilding and temple-building, on the other hand, do in a certain way make their own works. Here building, in contrast with cultivating, is a constructing. Both modes of building—building as cultivating, Latin *colere, cultura,* and building as the raising up of edifices, *aedificare*—are comprised within genuine building, that is, dwelling. Building as dwelling, that is, as being on the earth, however, remains for man's everyday experience that which is from the outset "habitual"—we inhabit it, as our language says so beautifully: it is the *Gewohnte.* For this reason it recedes behind the manifold ways in which dwelling is accomplished, the activities of cultivation and construction. These activities later claim the name of *bauen,* building, and with it the fact of building, exclusively for themselves. The real sense of *bauen,* namely dwelling, falls into oblivion.

At first sight this event looks as though it were no more than a change of meaning of mere terms. In truth, however, something decisive is concealed in it, namely, dwelling is not experienced as man's being; dwelling is never thought of as the basic character of human being.

That language in a way retracts the real meaning of the word *bauen,* which is dwelling, is evidence of the primal nature of these meanings; for with the essential words of language, their true meaning easily falls into oblivion in favor of foreground meanings. Man has hardly yet pondered the mystery of this process. Language withdraws from man its simple and high speech. But its primal call does not thereby become incapable of speech; it merely falls silent. Man, though, fails to heed this silence.

But if we listen to what language says in the word *bauen* we hear three things:

1. Building is really dwelling.
2. Dwelling is the manner in which mortals are on the earth.
3. Building as dwelling unfolds into the building that cultivates growing things and the building that erects buildings.

If we give thought to this threefold fact, we obtain a clue and note the following: as long as we do not bear in mind that all building is in itself a dwelling, we cannot even adequately *ask,* let alone properly decide, what the building of buildings might be in its nature. We do not dwell because we have built, but we build and have built because we dwell, that is, because we are *dwellers.* But in what does the nature of dwelling consist? Let us listen once more to what language says to us. The Old Saxon *wuon,* the Gothic *wunian,* like the old word *bauen,* mean to remain, to stay in a place. But the Gothic *wunian* says more distinctly how this remaining is experienced. *Wunian* means: to be at peace, to be brought to peace, to remain in peace. The word for peace, *Friede,* means the free, *das Frye,* and *fry* means: preserved from harm and danger, preserved from something, safeguarded. To free really means to spare. The sparing itself consists not only in the fact that we do not harm the one whom we spare. Real sparing is something *positive* and takes place when we leave something beforehand in its own nature, when we return it specifically to its being, when we "free" it in the real sense of the word into a preserve of peace. To dwell, to be set at peace, means to remain at peace within the free, the preserve, the free sphere that safeguards each thing in its nature. *The fundamental character of dwelling is this sparing and preserving.* It pervades dwelling in its whole range. That range reveals itself to us as soon as we reflect that human being consists in dwelling and, indeed, dwelling in the sense of the stay of mortals on the earth.

But "on the earth" already means "under the sky." Both of these *also* mean "remaining before the divinities" and include a "belonging to men's being with one another." By a *primal* oneness the four—earth and sky, divinities and mortals—belong together in one.

Earth is the serving bearer, blossoming and fruiting, spreading out in rock and water, rising up into plant and animal. When we say earth, we are already thinking of the other three along with it, but we give no thought to the simple oneness of the four.

The sky is the vaulting path of the sun, the course of the changing moon, the wandering glitter of the stars, the year's seasons and their changes, the light and dusk of day, the gloom and glow of night, the clemency and inclemency of the weather, the drifting clouds and blue depth of the ether. When we say sky, we are already thinking of the other three along with it, but we give no thought to the simple oneness of the four.

The divinities are the beckoning messengers of the godhead. Out of the holy sway of the godhead, the god appears in his presence or withdraws into his concealment. When we speak of the divinities, we are already thinking of the other three along with them, but we give no thought to the simple oneness of the four.

The mortals are the human beings. They are called mortals because they can die. To die means to be capable of death *as* death. Only man dies, and indeed continually, as long as he remains on earth, under the sky, before the divinities. When we speak of mortals, we are already thinking of the other three along with them, but we give no thought to the simple oneness of the four.

This simple oneness of the four we call *the fourfold*. Mortals *are* in the fourfold by *dwelling*. But the basic character of dwelling is to spare, to preserve. Mortals dwell in the way they preserve the fourfold in its essential being, its presencing. Accordingly, the preserving that dwells is fourfold.

Mortals dwell in that they save the earth—taking the word in the old sense still known to Lessing. Saving does not only snatch something from a danger. To save really means to set something free into its own presencing. To save the earth is more than to exploit it or even wear it out. Saving the earth does not master the earth and does not subjugate it, which is merely one step from spoliation.

Mortals dwell in that they receive the sky as sky. They leave to the sun and the moon their journey, to the stars their courses, to the seasons their blessing and their inclemency; they do not turn night into day nor day into a harassed unrest.

Mortals dwell in that they await the divinities as divinities. In hope they hold up to the divinities what is unhoped for. They wait for intimations of their coming and do not mistake the signs of their absence. They do not make their gods for themselves and do not worship idols. In the very depth of misfortune they wait for the weal that has been withdrawn.

Mortals dwell in that they initiate their own nature—their being capable of death as death—into the use and practice of this capacity, so that there may be a good death. To initiate mortals into the nature of death in no way means to make death, as empty Nothing, the goal. Nor does it mean to darken dwelling by blindly staring toward the end.

In saving the earth, in receiving the sky, in awaiting the divinities, in initiating mortals, dwelling occurs as the fourfold preservation of the fourfold. To spare and preserve means: to take under our care, to look after the fourfold in its presencing. What we take under our care must be kept safe. But if dwelling preserves the fourfold, where does it keep the fourfold's nature? How do mortals make their dwelling such a preserving? Mortals would never be capable of it if dwelling were merely a staying on earth under the sky, before the divinities, among mortals. Rather, dwelling itself is always a staying with things. Dwelling, as preserving, keeps the fourfold in that with which mortals stay: in things.

Staying with things, however, is not merely something attached to this fourfold preserving as a fifth something. On the contrary: staying with things is the only way in which the four-fold stay within the fourfold is accomplished at any time in simple unity. Dwelling preserves the fourfold by bringing the presencing of the fourfold into things. But things themselves secure the fourfold *only when* they themselves *as* things are let be in their presencing. How is this done? In this way, that mortals nurse and nurture the things that grow, and specially construct things that do not grow. Cultivating and construction are building in the narrower sense. *Dwelling,* insofar as it keeps or secures the fourfold in things, is, as this keeping, *a building.* With this, we are on our way to the second question.

II

In what way does building belong to dwelling?

The answer to this question will clarify for us what building, understood by way of the nature of dwelling, really is. We limit ourselves to building in the sense of constructing things and inquire: what is a built thing? A bridge may serve as an example for our reflections.

The bridge swings over the stream "with ease and power." It does not just connect banks that are already there. The banks emerge as banks only as the bridge crosses the stream. The bridge designedly causes them to lie across from each other. One side is set off against the other by the bridge. Nor do the banks stretch along the stream as indifferent border strips of the dry land. With the banks, the bridge brings to the stream the one and the other expanse of the landscape lying behind them. It brings stream and bank and land into each other's neighborhood. The bridge *gathers* the earth as landscape around the stream. Thus it guides and attends the stream through the meadows. Resting upright in the stream's bed, the bridge-piers bear the swing of the arches that leave the stream's waters to run their course. The waters may wander on quiet and gay, the sky's floods from storm or thaw may shoot past the piers in torrential waves—the bridge is ready for the sky's weather and its fickle nature. Even where the bridge covers the stream, it holds its flow up to the sky by taking it for a moment under the vaulted gateway and then setting it free once more.

The bridge lets the stream run its course and at the same time grants their way to mortals so that they may come and go from shore to shore. Bridges lead in many ways. The city bridge leads from the precincts of the castle to the cathedral square; the river bridge near the country town brings wagons and horse teams to the surrounding villages. The old stone bridge's humble brook crossing gives to the harvest wagon its passage from the fields into the village and carries the lumber cart from the field path to the road. The highway bridge is tied into the network of long-distance traffic, paced as calculated for maximum yield. Always and ever differently the bridge escorts the lingering and hastening ways of men to and fro, so that they may get to other banks and in the end, as mortals, to the other side. Now in a high arch, now in a low, the bridge vaults over glen and stream—whether mortals keep in mind this vaulting of the bridge's course or forget that they, always themselves on their way to the last bridge, are actually striving to surmount all that is common and unsound in them in order to bring themselves before the haleness of the divinities. The bridge *gathers,* as a passage that crosses, before the divinities—whether we explicitly think of, and visibly *give thanks for,* their presence, as in the figure of the saint of the bridge, or whether that divine presence is obstructed or even pushed wholly aside.

The bridge *gathers* to itself in *its own* way earth and sky, divinities and mortals.

Gathering or assembly, by an ancient word of our language, is called "thing." The bridge is a thing—and, indeed, it is such *as* the gathering of the fourfold which we have described. To be sure, people think of the bridge as primarily and really *merely* a bridge; after that, and occasionally, it might possibly express much else besides; and as such an expression it would then become a symbol, for instance a symbol of those things we mentioned before. But the bridge, if it is a true bridge, is never first of all a mere bridge and then afterward a symbol. And just as little is the bridge in the first place exclusively a symbol, in the sense that it expresses something that strictly speaking does not belong to it. If we take the bridge strictly as such, it never appears as an expression. The bridge is a thing and *only that.* Only? As this thing it gathers the fourfold.

Our thinking has of course long been accustomed to *understate* the nature of the thing. The consequence, in the course of Western thought, has been that the thing is represented as an unknown X to which perceptible properties are attached. From this point of view, everything *that already belongs to the gathering nature of this thing* does, of course, appear as something that is afterward read into it. Yet the bridge would never be a mere bridge if it were not a thing.

To be sure, the bridge is a thing of its *own* kind; for it gathers the fourfold in *such* a way that it allows a *site* for it. But only something *that is itself a location* can make space for a site. The location is not already there before the bridge is. Before the bridge stands, there are of course many spots along the stream that can be occupied by something. One of them proves to be a location, and does so *because of the bridge*. Thus the bridge does not first come to a location to stand in it; rather, a location comes into existence only by virtue of the bridge. The bridge is a thing; it gathers the fourfold, but in such a way that it allows a site for the fourfold. By this site are determined the localities and ways by which a space is provided for.

Only things that are locations in this manner allow for spaces. What the word for space, *Raum, Rum,* designates is said by its ancient meaning. *Raum* means a place cleared or freed for settlement and lodging. A space is something that has been made room for, something that is cleared and free, namely within a boundary, Greek *peras*. A boundary is not that at which something stops but, as the Greeks recognized, the boundary is that from which something *begins its presencing*. That is why the concept is that of *horismos*, that is, the horizon, the boundary. Space is in essence that for which room has been made, that which is let into its bounds. That for which room is made is always granted and hence is joined, that is, gathered, by virtue of a location, that is, by such a thing as the bridge. *Accordingly, spaces receive their being from locations and not from "space."*

Things which, as locations, allow a site we now in anticipation call buildings. They are so called because they are made by a process of building construction. Of what sort this making—building—must be, however, we find out only after we have first given thought to the nature of those things which of themselves require building as the process by which they are made. These things are locations that allow a site for the fourfold, a site that in each case provides for a space. The relation between location and space lies in the nature of these things *qua* locations, but so does the relation of the location to the man who lives at that location. Therefore we shall now try to clarify the nature of these things that we call buildings by the following brief consideration.

For one thing, what is the relation between location and space? For another, what is the relation between man and space?

The bridge is a location. As such a thing, it allows a space into which earth and heaven, divinities and mortals are admitted. The space allowed by the bridge contains many places variously near or far from the bridge. These places, however, may be treated as mere positions between which there lies a measurable distance; a distance, in Greek *stadion*, always has room made for it, and indeed by bare positions. The space that is thus made by positions is space of a peculiar sort. As distance or "stadion" it is what the same word, *stadion*, means in Latin, a *spatium*, an intervening space or interval. Thus nearness and remoteness between men and things can become mere distance, mere intervals of intervening space. In a space that is represented purely as *spatium*, the bridge now appears as a mere something at some position, which can be occupied at any time by something else or replaced by a mere marker. What is more, the mere dimensions of height, breadth, and depth can be abstracted from space as intervals. What is so abstracted we represent as the pure manifold of the three dimensions. Yet the room made by this manifold is also no longer determined by distances; it is no longer a *spatium*, but now no more than *extensio*— extension. But from space as *extensio* a further abstraction can be made, to analytic-algebraic relations. What these relations make room for is the possibility of the purely mathematical construction of manifolds with an arbitrary number of dimensions. The space provided for in this mathematical manner may be called "space," the "one" space as such. But in this sense "the" space, "space," contains no spaces and no places. We never find in it any locations, that is, things of the kind the bridge is. As against that, however, in the spaces provided for by locations there is always space as interval, and in this interval in turn there is space as pure extension. *Spatium* and *extensio* afford at any time the possibility of measuring things and what they make room for, according to distances, spans, and directions, and of computing these magnitudes. But the fact that they are *universally* applicable to everything that has extension can in no case make numerical magnitudes the *ground* of the nature of spaces and locations that are measurable with the aid of mathematics. How even modern physics was compelled by the facts themselves to represent the spatial medium of cosmic space as a field-unity determined by body as dynamic center, cannot be discussed here.

The spaces through which we go daily are provided for by locations; their nature is grounded in things of the type of buildings. If we pay heed to these relations between locations and spaces, between spaces and space, we get a clue to help us in thinking of the relation of man and space.

When we speak of man and space, it sounds as though man stood on one side, space on the other. Yet space is not something that faces man. It is neither an external object nor an inner experience. It is not that there are men, and over and above them *space;* for when I say "a man," and in saying this word think of a being who exists in a human manner—that is, who dwells—then by the name "man" I already name the stay within the fourfold among things. Even when we relate ourselves to those things that are not in our immediate reach, we are staying with the things themselves. We do not represent distant things merely in our mind—as the textbooks have it—so that only mental representations of distant things run through our minds and heads as substitutes for the things. If all of us now think, from where we are right here, of the old bridge in Heidelberg, this thinking toward that location is not a mere experience inside the persons present here; rather, it belongs to the nature of our thinking *of* that bridge that *in itself* thinking gets through, persists through, the distance to that location.

From this spot right here, we are there at the bridge—we are by no means at some representational content in our consciousness. From right here we may even be much nearer to that bridge and to what it makes room for than someone who uses it daily as an indifferent river crossing. Spaces, and with them space as such—"space"—are always provided for already within the stay of mortals. Spaces open up by the fact that they are let into the dwelling of man. To say that mortals *are* is to say that *in dwelling* they persist through spaces by virtue of their stay among things and locations. And only because mortals pervade, persist through, spaces by their very nature are they able to go through spaces. But in going through spaces we do not give up our standing in them. Rather, we always go through spaces in such a way that we already experience them by staying constantly with near and remote locations and things. When I go toward the door of the lecture hall, I am already there, and I could not go to it at all if I were not such that I am there. I am never here only, as this encapsulated body; rather, I am there, that is, I already pervade the room, and only thus can I go through it.

Even when mortals turn "inward," taking stock of themselves, they do not leave behind their belonging to the fourfold. When, as we say, we come to our senses and reflect on ourselves, we come back to ourselves from things *without ever abandoning* our stay among things. Indeed, the loss of rapport with things that occurs in states of depression would be wholly impossible if even such a state were not still what it is as a human state: that is, a staying *with* things. Only if this stay already characterizes human being can the things among which we are also *fail* to speak to us, *fail* to concern us any longer.

Man's relation to locations, and through locations to spaces, inheres in his dwelling. The relationship between man and space is none other than dwelling, strictly thought and spoken.

When we think, in the manner just attempted, about the relation between location and space, but also about the relation of man and space, a light falls on the nature of the things that are locations and that we call buildings.

The bridge is a thing of this sort. The location allows the simple onefold of earth and sky, of divinities and mortals, to enter into a site by arranging the site into spaces. The location makes room for the fourfold in a double sense. The location *admits* the fourfold and it *installs* the fourfold. The two—making room in the sense of admitting and in the sense of installing—belong together. As a double space-making, the location is a shelter for the fourfold or, by the same token, a house. Things like such locations shelter or house men's lives. Things of this sort are housings, though not necessarily dwelling-houses in the narrower sense.

The making of such things is building. Its nature consists in this, that it corresponds to the character of these things. They are locations that allow spaces. This is why building, by virtue of constructing locations, is a founding and joining of spaces. Because building produces locations, the joining of the spaces of these locations necessarily brings with it space, as *spatium* and as *extensio,* into the thingly structure of buildings. But building never shapes pure "space" as a single entity. Neither directly nor indirectly. Nevertheless, because it produces things as locations, building is closer to the nature of spaces and to the origin of the nature of "space" than any geometry and mathematics. Building puts up locations that make space and a site for the fourfold. From the simple oneness in which earth and sky, divinities and mortals belong together, building *receives the directive* for its erecting of locations. Building *takes over* from the fourfold the standard for all the traversing and measuring of the spaces that in each case are provided for by the locations that have been founded. The edifices guard the fourfold. They are things that in their own way preserve the fourfold. To preserve the fourfold, to save the earth, to receive the sky, to await the divinities, to escort mortals—this fourfold preserving is the simple nature, the presencing, of dwelling. In this way, then, do genuine buildings give form to dwelling in its presencing and house this presence.

Building thus characterized is a distinctive letting-dwell. Whenever it *is* such in fact, building already *has* responded to the summons of the fourfold. All planning remains grounded on this responding, and planning in turn opens up to the designer the precincts suitable for his designs.

As soon as we try to think of the nature of constructive building in terms of a letting-dwell, we come to know more clearly what that process of making consists in by which building is accomplished. Usually we take production to be an activity whose performance has a result, the finished structure, as its consequence. It is possible to conceive of making in that way; we thereby grasp something that is correct, and yet never touch its nature, which is a producing that brings something forth. For building brings the fourfold *hither* into a thing, the bridge, and brings *forth* the thing as a location, out into what is already there, room for which is only now made *by* this location.

The Greek for "to bring forth or to produce" is *tikto*. The word *techne,* technique, belongs to the verb's root *tec.* To the Greeks *techne* means neither art nor handicraft but rather: to make something appear, within what is present, as this or that, in this way or that way. The Greeks conceive of *techne,* producing, in terms of letting appear. *Techne* thus conceived has been concealed in the tectonics of architecture since ancient times. Of late it still remains concealed, and more resolutely, in the technology of power machinery. But the nature of the erecting of buildings cannot be understood adequately in terms either of architecture or of engineering construction, nor in terms of a mere combination of the two. The erecting of buildings would not be suitably defined *even if* we were to think of it in the sense of the original Greek *techne* as *solely* a letting-appear, which brings something made, as something present, among the things that are already present.

The nature of building is letting dwell. Building accomplishes its nature in the raising of locations by the joining of their spaces. *Only if we are capable of dwelling, only then can we build.* Let us think for a while of a farmhouse in the Black Forest, which was built some two hundred years ago by the dwelling of peasants. Here the self-sufficiency of the power to let earth and heaven, divinities and mortals enter *in simple oneness* into things, ordered the house. It placed the farm on the wind-sheltered mountain slope looking south, among the meadows close to the spring. It gave it the wide overhanging shingle roof whose proper slope bears up under the burden of snow, and which, reaching deep down, shields the chambers against the storms of the long winter nights. It did not forget the altar corner behind the community table; it made room in its chamber for the hallowed places of childbed and the "tree of the dead"—for that is what they call a coffin there: the *Totenbaum*—and in this way it designed for the different generations under one roof the character of their journey through time. A craft which, itself sprung from dwelling, still uses its tools and frames as things, built the farmhouse.

Only if we are capable of dwelling, only then can we build. Our reference to the Black Forest farm in no way means that we should or could go back to building such houses; rather, it illustrates by a dwelling that *has been* how *it* was able to build.

Dwelling, however, is *the basic character* of Being in keeping with which mortals exist. Perhaps this attempt to think about dwelling and building will bring out somewhat more clearly that building belongs to dwelling and how it receives its nature from dwelling. Enough will have been gained if dwelling and building have become *worthy of questioning* and thus have remained *worthy of thought*.

But that thinking itself belongs to dwelling in the same sense as building, although in a different way, may perhaps be attested to by the course of thought here attempted.

Building and thinking are, each in its own way, inescapable

for dwelling. The two, however, are also insufficient for dwelling so long as each busies itself with its own affairs in separation instead of listening to one another. They are able to listen if both—building and thinking—belong to dwelling, if they remain within their limits and realize that the one as much as the other comes from the workshop of long experience and incessant practice.

We are attempting to trace in thought the nature of dwelling. The next step on this path would be the question: what is the state of dwelling in our precarious age? On all sides we hear talk about the housing shortage, and with good reason. Nor is there just talk; there is action too. We try to fill the need by providing houses, by promoting the building of houses, planning the whole architectural enterprise. However hard and bitter, however hampering and threatening the lack of houses remains, the *real plight of dwelling* does not lie merely in a lack of houses. The real plight of dwelling is indeed older than the world wars with their destruction, older also than the increase of the earth's population and the condition of the industrial workers. The real dwelling plight lies in this, that mortals ever search anew for the nature of dwelling, that they *must ever learn to dwell.* What if man's homelessness consisted in this, that man still does not even think of the *real* plight of dwelling as *the* plight? Yet as soon as man *gives thought* to his homelessness, it is a misery no longer. Rightly considered and kept well in mind, it is the sole summons that *calls* mortals into their dwelling.

But how else can mortals answer this summons than by trying on *their* part, on their own, to bring dwelling to the fullness of its nature? This they accomplish when they build out of dwelling, and think for the sake of dwelling.

THE THING

THE THING

All distances in time and space are shrinking. Man now reaches overnight, by plane, places which formerly took weeks and months of travel. He now receives instant information, by radio, of events which he formerly learned about only years later, if at all. The germination and growth of plants, which remained hidden throughout the seasons, is now exhibited publicly in a minute, on film. Distant sites of the most ancient cultures are shown on film as if they stood this very moment amidst today's street traffic. Moreover, the film attests to what it shows by presenting also the camera and its operators at work. The peak of this abolition of every possibility of remoteness is reached by television, which will soon pervade and dominate the whole machinery of communication.

Man puts the longest distances behind him in the shortest time. He puts the greatest distances behind himself and thus puts everything before himself at the shortest range.

Yet the frantic abolition of all distances brings no nearness; for nearness does not consist in shortness of distance. What is least remote from us in point of distance, by virtue of its picture on film or its sound on the radio, can remain far from us. What is incalculably far from us in point of distance can be near to us. Short distance is not in itself nearness. Nor is great distance remoteness.

What is nearness if it fails to come about despite the reduction of the longest distances to the shortest intervals? What is nearness if it is even repelled by the restless abolition of distances? What is nearness if, along with its failure to appear, remoteness also remains absent?

What is happening here when, as a result of the abolition of great distances, everything is equally far and equally near? What is this uniformity in which everything is neither far nor near—is, as it were, without distance?

Everything gets lumped together into uniform distancelessness. How? Is not this merging of everything into the distanceless more unearthly than everything bursting apart?

Man stares at what the explosion of the atom bomb could bring with it. He does not see that the atom bomb and its explosion are the mere final emission of what has long since taken place, has already happened. Not to mention the single hydrogen bomb, whose triggering, thought through to its utmost potential, might be enough to snuff out all life on earth. What is this helpless anxiety still waiting for, if the terrible has already happened?

The terrifying is unsettling; it places everything outside its own nature. What is it that unsettles and thus terrifies? It shows itself and hides itself in the *way* in which everything presences, namely, in the fact that despite all conquest of distances the nearness of things remains absent.

What about nearness? How can we come to know its nature? Nearness, it seems, cannot be encountered directly. We succeed in reaching it rather by attending to what is near. Near to us are what we usually call things. But what is a thing? Man has so far given no more thought to the thing as a thing than he has to nearness. The jug is a thing. What is the jug? We say: a vessel, something of the kind that holds something else within it. The jug's holding is done by its base and sides. This container itself can again be held by the handle. As a vessel the jug is something self-sustained, something that stands on its own. This standing on its own characterizes the jug as something that is self-supporting, or independent. As the self-supporting independence of something independent, the jug differs from an object. An independent, self-supporting thing may become an object if we place it before us, whether in immediate perception or by bringing it to mind in a recollective re-presentation. However, the thingly character of the thing does not consist in its being a represented object, nor can it be defined in any way in terms of the objectness, the over-againstness, of the object.

The jug remains a vessel whether we represent it in our minds or not. As a vessel the jug stands on its own as self-supporting. But what does it mean to say that the container stands on its own? Does the vessel's self-support alone define the jug as a thing? Clearly the jug stands as a vessel only because it has been brought to a stand. This happened during, and happens by means of, a process of setting, of setting forth, namely, by producing the jug. The potter makes the earthen jug out of earth that he has specially chosen and prepared for it. The jug consists of that earth. By virtue of what the jug consists of, it too can stand on the earth, either immediately or through the mediation of table and bench. What exists by such producing is what stands on its own, is self-supporting. When we take the jug as a made vessel, then surely we are apprehending it—so it seems—as a thing and never as a mere object.

Or do we even now still take the jug as an object? Indeed. It is, to be sure, no longer considered only an object of a mere act of representation, but in return it is an object which a process of making has set up before and against us. Its self-support seems to mark the jug as a thing. But in truth we are thinking of this self-support in terms of the making process. Self-support is what the making aims at. But even so, the self-support is still thought of in terms of objectness, even though the over-againstness of what has been put forth is no longer grounded in mere representation, in the mere putting it before our minds. But from the objectness of the object, and from the product's self-support, there is no way that leads to the thingness of the thing.

What in the thing is thingly? What is the thing in itself? We shall not reach the thing in itself until our thinking has first reached the thing as a thing.

The jug is a thing as a vessel—it can hold something. To be sure, this container has to be made. But its being made by the potter in no way constitutes what is peculiar and proper to the jug insofar as it is *qua* jug. The jug is not a vessel because it was made; rather, the jug had to be made because it is this holding vessel.

The making, it is true, lets the jug come into its own. But that which in the jug's nature is its own is never brought about by its making. Now released from the making process, the self-supporting jug has to gather itself for the task of containing. In the process of its making, of course, the jug must first show its outward appearance to the maker. But what shows itself here, the aspect (the *eidos,* the *idea*), characterizes the jug solely in the respect in which the vessel stands over against the maker as something to be made.

But what the vessel of this aspect *is* as this jug, what and how the jug *is* as this jug-thing, is something we can never learn—let alone think properly—by looking at the outward appearance, the *idea.* That is why Plato, who conceives of the presence of what is present in terms of the outward appearance, had no more understanding of the nature of the thing than did Aristotle and all subsequent thinkers. Rather, Plato experienced (decisively, indeed, for the sequel) everything present as an object of making. Instead of "object"—as that which stands before, over against, opposite us—we use the more precise expression "what stands forth." In the full nature of what stands forth, a twofold standing prevails. First, standing forth has the sense of stemming from somewhere, whether this be a process of self-making or of being made by another. Secondly, standing forth has the sense of the made thing's standing forth into the unconcealedness of what is already present.

Nevertheless, no representation of what is present, in the sense of what stands forth and of what stands over against as an object, ever reaches to the thing *qua* thing. The jug's thing-ness resides in its being *qua* vessel. We become aware of the vessel's holding nature when we fill the jug. The jug's bottom and sides obviously take on the task of holding. But not so fast! When we fill the jug with wine, do we pour the wine into the sides and bottom? At most, we pour the wine between the sides and over the bottom. Sides and bottom are, to be sure, what is impermeable in the vessel. But what is impermeable is not yet what does the holding. When we fill the jug, the pour-ing that fills it flows into the empty jug. The emptiness, the void, is what does the vessel's holding. The empty space, this nothing of the jug, is what the jug is as the holding vessel.

But the jug does consist of sides and bottom. By that of which the jug consists, it stands. What would a jug be that did not stand? At least a jug *manqué,* hence a jug still—namely, one that would indeed hold but that, constantly falling over, would empty itself of what it holds. Only a vessel, however, can empty itself.

Sides and bottom, of which the jug consists and by which it stands, are not really what does the holding. But if the holding is done by the jug's void, then the potter who forms sides and bottom on his wheel does not, strictly speaking, make the jug. He only shapes the clay. No—he shapes the void. For it, in it, and out of it, he forms the clay into the form. From start to finish the potter takes hold of the impalpable void and brings it forth as the container in the shape of a containing vessel. The jug's void determines all the handling in the process of making the vessel. The vessel's thingness does not lie at all in the material of which it consists, but in the void that holds.

And yet, is the jug really empty?

Physical science assures us that the jug is filled with air and with everything that goes to make up the air's mixture. We allowed ourselves to be misled by a semipoetic way of looking at things when we pointed to the void of the jug in order to define its acting as a container.

But as soon as we agree to study the actual jug scientifically, in regard to its reality, the facts turn out differently. When we pour wine into the jug, the air that already fills the jug is simply displaced by a liquid. Considered scientifically, to fill a jug means to exchange one filling for another.

These statements of physics are correct. By means of them, science represents something real, by which it is objectively controlled. But—is this reality the jug? No. Science always encounters only what *its* kind of representation has admitted beforehand as an object possible for science.

It is said that scientific knowledge is compelling. Certainly. But what does its compulsion consist in? In our instance it consists in the compulsion to relinquish the wine-filled jug and to put in its place a hollow within which a liquid spreads. Science makes the jug-thing into a nonentity in not permitting things to be the standard for what is real.

Science's knowledge, which is compelling within its own sphere, the sphere of objects, already had annihilated things as things long before the atom bomb exploded. The bomb's explosion is only the grossest of all gross confirmations of the long-since-accomplished annihilation of the thing: the confirmation that the thing as a thing remains nil. The thingness of the thing remains concealed, forgotten. The nature of the thing never comes to light, that is, it never gets a hearing. This is the meaning of our talk about the annihilation of the thing. That annihilation is so weird because it carries before it a twofold delusion: first, the notion that science is superior to all other experience in reaching the real in its reality, and second, the illusion that, notwithstanding the scientific investigation of reality, things could still be things, which would presuppose that they had once been in full possession of their thinghood. But if things ever had already shown themselves *qua* things in their thingness, then the thing's thingness would have become manifest and would have laid claim to thought. In truth, however, the thing as thing remains proscribed, nil, and in that sense annihilated. This has happened and continues to happen so essentially that not only are things no longer admitted as things, but they have never yet at all been able to appear to thinking as things.

To what is the nonappearance of the thing as thing due? Is it simply that man has neglected to represent the thing as thing to himself? Man can neglect only what has already been assigned to him. Man can represent, no matter how, only what has previously come to light of its own accord and has shown itself to him in the light it brought with it.

What, then, is the thing as thing, that its essential nature has never yet been able to appear?

Has the thing never yet come near enough for man to learn how to attend sufficiently to the thing as thing? What is nearness? We have already asked this question before. To learn what nearness is, we examined the jug near by.

In what does the jug-character of the jug consist? We suddenly lost sight of it—at the moment, in fact, when the illusion intruded itself that science could reveal to us the reality of the jug. We represented the effective feature of the vessel, that which does its holding, the void, as a hollow filled with air. Conceived in terms of physical science, that is what the void really is; but it is not the jug's void. We did not let the jug's void be *its* own void. We paid no heed to that in the vessel which does the containing. We have given no thought to how the containing itself goes on. Accordingly, even what the jug contains was bound to escape us. In the scientific view, the wine became a liquid, and liquidity in turn became one of the states of aggregation of matter, possible everywhere. We failed to give thought to what the jug holds and how it holds.

How does the jug's void hold? It holds by taking what is poured in. It holds by keeping and retaining what it took in. The void holds in a twofold manner: taking and keeping. The word "hold" is therefore ambiguous. Nevertheless, the taking of what is poured in and the keeping of what was poured belong together. But their unity is determined by the outpouring for which the jug is fitted as a jug. The twofold holding of the void rests on the outpouring. In the outpouring, the holding is authentically how it is. To pour from the jug is to give. The holding of the vessel occurs in the giving of the outpouring. Holding needs the void as that which holds. The nature of the holding void is gathered in the giving. But giving is richer than a mere pouring out. The giving, whereby the jug is a jug, gathers in the twofold holding—in the outpouring. We call the gathering of the twofold holding into the outpouring, which, as a being together, first constitutes the full presence of giving: the poured gift. The jug's jug-character consists in the poured gift of the pouring out. Even the empty jug retains its nature by virtue of the poured gift, even though the empty jug does not admit of a giving out. But this nonadmission belongs to the jug and to it alone. A scythe, by contrast, or a hammer is incapable of a nonadmission of this giving.

The giving of the outpouring can be a drink. The outpouring gives water, it gives wine to drink.

The spring stays on in the water of the gift. In the spring the rock dwells, and in the rock dwells the dark slumber of the earth, which receives the rain and dew of the sky. In the water of the spring dwells the marriage of sky and earth. It stays in the wine given by the fruit of the vine, the fruit in which the earth's nourishment and the sky's sun are betrothed to one another. In the gift of water, in the gift of wine, sky and earth dwell. But the gift of the outpouring is what makes the jug a jug. In the jugness of the jug, sky and earth dwell.

The gift of the pouring out is drink for mortals. It quenches their thirst. It refreshes their leisure. It enlivens their conviviality. But the jug's gift is at times also given for consecration. If the pouring is for consecration, then it does not still a thirst. It stills and elevates the celebration of the feast. The gift of the pouring now is neither given in an inn nor is the poured gift a drink for mortals. The outpouring is the libation poured out for the immortal gods. The gift of the outpouring as libation is

the authentic gift. In giving the consecrated libation, the pouring jug occurs as the giving gift. The consecrated libation is
what our word for a strong outpouring flow, "gush," really
designates: gift and sacrifice. "Gush," Middle English *guschen,*
gosshen—cf. German *Guss, giessen—*is the Greek *cheein,* the
Indoeuropean *ghu.* It means to offer in sacrifice. To pour a
gush, when it is achieved in its essence, thought through with
sufficient generosity, and genuinely uttered, is to donate, to offer
in sacrifice, and hence to give. It is only for this reason that the
pouring of the gush, once its nature withers, can become a mere
pouring in and pouring out, until it finally decays into the dis-
pensing of liquor at the bar. Pouring the outpour is not a mere
filling and decanting.

In the gift of the outpouring that is drink, mortals stay in
their own way. In the gift of the outpouring that is a libation,
the divinities stay in their own way, they who receive back the
gift of giving as the gift of the donation. In the gift of the
outpouring, mortals and divinities each dwell in their different
ways. Earth and sky dwell in the gift of the outpouring. In the
gift of the outpouring earth and sky, divinities and mortals
dwell *together all at once.* These four, at one because of what
they themselves are, belong together. Preceding everything that
is present, they are enfolded into a single fourfold.

In the gift of the outpouring dwells the simple singlefoldness
of the four.*

The gift of the outpouring is a gift because it stays earth
and sky, divinities and mortals. Yet staying is now no longer
the mere persisting of something that is here. Staying appropriates. It brings the four into the light of their mutual belonging. From out of staying's simple onefoldness they are betrothed,
entrusted to one another. At one in thus being entrusted to one
another, they are unconcealed. The gift of the outpouring stays
the onefold of the fourfold of the four. And in the poured gift
the jug presences as jug. The gift gathers what belongs to giving: the twofold containing, the container, the void, and the

* The German *Einfalt* means simplicity, literally onefoldedness.—Tr.

outpouring as donation. What is gathered in the gift gathers itself in appropriatively staying the fourfold. This manifold-simple gathering is the jug's presencing. Our language denotes what a gathering *is* by an ancient word. That word is: thing. The jug's presencing is the pure, giving gathering of the one-fold fourfold into a single time-space, a single stay. The jug presences as a thing. The jug is the jug as a thing. But how does the thing presence? The thing things. Thinging gathers. Appropriating the fourfold, it gathers the fourfold's stay, its while, into something that stays for a while: into this thing, that thing.

The jug's essential nature, its presencing, so experienced and thought of in these terms, is what we call *thing*. We are now thinking this word by way of the gathering-appropriating staying of the fourfold. At the same time we recall the Old High German word *thing*. This reference to the history of language could easily tempt us to misunderstand the way in which we are now thinking of the nature of the thing. It might look as though the nature of the thing as we are now thinking of it had been, so to speak, thoughtlessly poked out of the accidentally encountered meaning of the Old High German *thing*. The suspicion arises that the understanding of the nature of the thingness that we are here trying to reach may be based on the accidents of an etymological game. The notion becomes established and is already current that, instead of giving thought to essential matters, we are here merely using the dictionary.

The opposite is true. To be sure, the Old High German word *thing* means a gathering, and specifically a gathering to deliberate on a matter under discussion, a contested matter. In consequence, the Old German words *thing* and *dinc* become the names for an affair or matter of pertinence. They denote anything that in any way bears upon men, concerns them, and that accordingly is a matter for discourse. The Romans called a matter for discourse *res*. The Greek *eiro* (*rhetos, rhetra, rhema*) means to speak about something, to deliberate on it. *Res publica* means, not the state, but that which, known to everyone, concerns everybody and is therefore deliberated in public.

Only because *res* means what concerns men are the combinations *res adversae, res secundae* possible. The first is what affects or bears on man adversely, the second what attends man favorably. The dictionaries, to be sure, translate *res adversae* correctly as bad fortune, *res secundae* as good fortune; but dictionaries have little to report about what words, spoken thoughtfully, say. The truth, then, here and elsewhere, is not that our thinking feeds on etymology, but rather that etymology has the standing mandate first to give thought to the essential content involved in what dictionary words, as words, denote by implication.

The Roman word *res* designates that which concerns somebody, an affair, a contested matter, a case at law. The Romans also use for it the word *causa*. In its authentic and original sense, this word in no way signifies "cause"; *causa* means the case and hence also that which is the case, in the sense that something comes to pass and becomes due. Only because *causa*, almost synonymously with *res,* means the case, can the word *causa* later come to mean cause, in the sense of the causality of an effect. The Old German word *thing* or *dinc,* with its meaning of a gathering specifically for the purpose of dealing with a case or matter, is suited as no other word to translate properly the Roman word *res,* that which is pertinent, which has a bearing. From that word of the Roman language, which there corresponds to the word *res*—from the word *causa* in the sense of case, affair, matter of pertinence—there develop in turn the Romance *la cosa* and the French *la chose;* we say, "the thing." In English "thing" has still preserved the full semantic power of the Roman word: "He knows his things," he understands the matters that have a bearing on him; "He knows how to handle things," he knows how to go about dealing with affairs, that is, with what matters from case to case; "That's a great thing," that is something grand (fine, tremendous, splendid), something that comes of itself and bears upon man.

But the decisive point now is not at all the short semantic history here given of the words *res, Ding, causa, cosa, chose,* and *thing,* but something altogether different, to which no thought whatever has hitherto been given. The Roman word *res* denotes what pertains to man, concerns him and his interests in any way or manner. That which concerns man is what is real in *res.* The Roman experience of the *realitas* of *res* is that of a bearing-upon, a concern. But the Romans never properly thought through the nature of what they thus experienced. Rather, the Roman *realitas* of *res* is conceived in terms of the meaning of *on* which they took over from late Greek philosophy; *on,* Latin *ens,* means that which is present in the sense of standing forth here. *Res* becomes *ens,* that which is present in the sense of what is put here, put before us, presented. The peculiar *realitas* of *res* as originally experienced by the Romans, a bearing-upon or concern, i.e., the very nature of that which is present, remains buried. Conversely, in later times, especially in the Middle Ages, the term *res* serves to designate every *ens qua ens,* that is, everything present in any way whatever, even if it stands forth and presences only in mental representation as an *ens rationis.* The same happens with the corresponding term *thing* or *dinc;* for these words denote anything whatever that is in any way. Accordingly Meister Eckhart uses the word *thing* (*dinc*) for God as well as for the soul. God is for him the "highest and uppermost thing." The soul is a "great thing." This master of thinking in no way means to say that God and the soul are something like a rock: a material object. *Thing* is here the cautious and abstemious name for something that is at all. Thus Meister Eckhart says, adopting an expression of Dionysius the Areopagite: *diu minne ist der natur, daz si den menschen wandelt in die dinc, di er minnet*—love is of such a nature that it changes man into the things he loves.

Because the word *thing* as used in Western metaphysics denotes that which is at all and is something in some way or other, the meaning of the name "thing'" varies with the interpretation of that which is—of entities. Kant talks about things in the same way as Meister Eckhart and means by this term something that is. But for Kant, that which is becomes the object of a representing that runs its course in the self-consciousness of the human ego. The thing-in-itself means for Kant: the object-in-itself. To Kant, the character of the "in-itself" signifies that the object is an object in itself without reference to the human act of representing it, that is, without the opposing "ob-" by which it is first of all put before this representing act. "Thing-in-itself," thought in a rigorously Kantian way, means an object that is no object for us, because it is supposed to stand, stay put, without a possible before: for the human representational act that encounters it.

Neither the general, long outworn meaning of the term "thing," as used in philosophy, nor the Old High German meaning of the word *thing,* however, are of the least help to us in our pressing need to discover and give adequate thought to the essential source of what we are now saying about the nature of the jug. However, *one* semantic factor in the old usage of the word *thing,* namely "gathering," does speak to the nature of the jug as we earlier had it in mind.

The jug is a thing neither in the sense of the Roman *res,* nor in the sense of the medieval *ens,* let alone in the modern sense of object. The jug is a thing insofar as it things. The presence of something present such as the jug comes into its own, appropriatively manifests and determines itself, only from the thinging of the thing.

Today everything present is equally near and equally far. The distanceless prevails. But no abridging or abolishing of distances brings nearness. What is nearness? To discover the nature of nearness, we gave thought to the jug near by. We have sought the nature of nearness and found the nature of the jug as a thing. But in this discovery we also catch sight of the nature of nearness. The thing things. In thinging, it stays earth and sky, divinities and mortals. Staying, the thing brings the four, in their remoteness, near to one another. This bringing-near is nearing. Nearing is the presencing of nearness. Nearness brings near—draws nigh to one another—the far and, indeed, *as* the far. Nearness preserves farness. Preserving farness, nearness presences nearness in nearing that farness. Bringing near in this way, nearness conceals its own self and remains, in its own way, nearest of all.

The thing is not "in" nearness, "in" proximity, as if nearness were a container. Nearness is at work in bringing near, as the thinging of the thing.

Thinging, the thing stays the united four, earth and sky, divinities and mortals, in the simple onefold of their self-unified fourfold.

Earth is the building bearer, nourishing with its fruits, tending water and rock, plant and animal.

When we say earth, we are already thinking of the other three along with it by way of the simple oneness of the four.

The sky is the sun's path, the course of the moon, the glitter of the stars, the year's seasons, the light and dusk of day, the gloom and glow of night, the clemency and inclemency of the weather, the drifting clouds and blue depth of the ether.

When we say sky, we are already thinking of the other three along with it by way of the simple oneness of the four.

The divinities are the beckoning messengers of the godhead. Out of the hidden sway of the divinities the god emerges as what he is, which removes him from any comparison with beings that are present.

When we speak of the divinities, we are already thinking of the other three along with them by way of the simple oneness of the four.

The mortals are human beings. They are called mortals because they can die. To die means to be capable of death as death. Only man dies. The animal perishes. It has death neither ahead of itself nor behind it. Death is the shrine of Nothing, that is, of that which in every respect is never something that merely exists, but which nevertheless presences, even as the mystery of Being itself. As the shrine of Nothing, death harbors within itself the presencing of Being. As the shrine of Nothing, death is the shelter of Being. We now call mortals mortals— not because their earthly life comes to an end, but because they are capable of death as death. Mortals are who they are, as mortals, present in the shelter of Being. They are the presencing relation to Being as Being.

Metaphysics, by contrast, thinks of man as *animal,* as a living being. Even when *ratio* pervades *animalitas,* man's being re- mains defined by life and life-experience. Rational living beings must first *become* mortals.

When we say mortals, we are then thinking of the other three along with them by way of the simple oneness of the four.

Earth and sky, divinities and mortals—being at one with one another of their own accord—belong together by way of the simpleness of the united fourfold. Each of the four mirrors in its own way the presence of the others. Each therewith reflects itself in its own way into its own, within the simpleness of the four. This mirroring does not portray a likeness. The mirroring, lightening each of the four, appropriates their own presencing into simple belonging to one another. Mirroring in this appro- priating-lightening way, each of the four plays to each of the others. The appropriative mirroring sets each of the four free into its own, but it binds these free ones into the simplicity of their essential being toward one another.

The mirroring that binds into freedom is the play that be- troths each of the four to each through the enfolding clasp of their mutual appropriation. None of the four insists on its own separate particularity. Rather, each is expropriated, within their mutual appropriation, into its own being. This expropriative appropriating is the mirror-play of the fourfold. Out of the fourfold, the simple onefold of the four is ventured.

This appropriating mirror-play of the simple onefold of earth and sky, divinities and mortals, we call the world. The world presences by worlding. That means: the world's worlding cannot be explained by anything else nor can it be fathomed through anything else. This impossibility does not lie in the inability of our human thinking to explain and fathom in this way. Rather, the inexplicable and unfathomable character of the world's worlding lies in this, that causes and grounds remain unsuitable for the world's worlding. As soon as human cognition here calls for an explanation, it fails to transcend the world's nature, and falls short of it. The human will to explain just does not reach to the simpleness of the simple onefold of worlding. The united four are already strangled in their essential nature when we think of them only as separate realities, which are to be grounded in and explained by one another.

The unity of the fourfold is the fouring. But the fouring does not come about in such a way that it encompasses the four and only afterward is added to them as that compass. Nor does the fouring exhaust itself in this, that the four, once they are there, stand side by side singly.

The fouring, the unity of the four, presences as the appropriating mirror-play of the betrothed, each to the other in simple oneness. The fouring presences as the worlding of world. The mirror-play of world is the round dance of appropriating. Therefore, the round dance does not encompass the four like a hoop. The round dance is the ring that joins while it plays as mirroring. Appropriating, it lightens the four into the radiance of their simple oneness. Radiantly, the ring joins the four, everywhere open to the riddle of their presence. The gathered presence of the mirror-play of the world, joining in this way, is the ringing. In the ringing of the mirror-playing ring, the four nestle into their unifying presence, in which each one retains its own nature. So nestling, they join together, worlding, the world.

Nestling, malleable, pliant, compliant, nimble—in Old German these are called *ring* and *gering*. The mirror-play of the worlding world, as the ringing of the ring, wrests free the united four into their own compliancy, the circling compliancy of their presence. Out of the ringing mirror-play the thinging of the thing takes place.

The thing stays—gathers and unites—the fourfold. The thing things world. Each thing stays the fourfold into a happening of the simple onehood of world.

If we let the thing be present in its thinging from out of the worlding world, then we are thinking of the thing as thing. Taking thought in this way, we let ourselves be concerned by the thing's worlding being. Thinking in this way, we are called by the thing as the thing. In the strict sense of the German word *bedingt,* we are the be-thinged, the conditioned ones. We have left behind us the presumption of all unconditionedness.

If we think of the thing as thing, then we spare and protect the thing's presence in the region from which it presences. Thinging is the nearing of world. Nearing is the nature of nearness. As we preserve the thing *qua* thing we inhabit nearness. The nearing of nearness is the true and sole dimension of the mirror-play of the world.

The failure of nearness to materialize in consequence of the abolition of all distances has brought the distanceless to dominance. In the default of nearness the thing remains annihilated as a thing in our sense. But when and in what way do things exist as things? This is the question we raise in the midst of the dominance of the distanceless.

When and in what way do things appear as things? They do not appear *by means of* human making. But neither do they appear without the vigilance of mortals. The first step toward such vigilance is the step back from the thinking that merely represents—that is, explains—to the thinking that responds and recalls.

The step back from the one thinking to the other is no mere shift of attitude. It can never be any such thing for this reason alone: that all attitudes, including the ways in which they shift, remain committed to the precincts of representational thinking. The step back does, indeed, depart from the sphere of mere attitudes. The step back takes up its residence in a co-responding which, appealed to in the world's being by the world's being, answers within itself to that appeal. A mere shift of attitude is powerless to bring about the advent of the thing as thing, just as nothing that stands today as an object in the distanceless can ever be simply switched over into a thing. Nor do things as things ever come about if we merely avoid objects and recollect former objects which perhaps were once on the way to becoming things and even to actually presencing as things.

Whatever becomes a thing occurs out of the ringing of the world's mirror-play. Only when—all of a sudden, presumaby— world worlds as a world, only then does the ring shine forth, the joining from which the ringing of earth and heaven, divinities and mortals, wrests itself free for that compliancy of simple oneness.

In accordance with this ring thinging itself is unpretentious, and each present thing, modestly compliant, fits into its own being. Inconspicuously compliant is the thing: the jug and the bench, the footbridge and the plow. But tree and pond, too, brook and hill, are things, each in its own way. Things, each thinging from time to time in its own way, are heron and roe, deer, horse and bull. Things, each thinging and each staying in its own way, are mirror and clasp, book and picture, crown and cross.

But things are also compliant and modest in number, compared with the countless objects everywhere of equal value, compared with the measureless mass of men as living beings.

Men alone, as mortals, by dwelling attain to the world as world. Only what conjoins itself out of world becomes a thing.

Epilogue

Freiburg i. Br., 18. June 1950

DEAR MR. BUCHNER:

Thank you for your letter. Your questions are important and your argumentation is correct. Nevertheless it remains to consider whether they touch on what is decisive.

You ask: whence does thinking about Being receive (to speak concisely) its directive?

Here you are not considering "Being" as an object, nor thinking as the mere activity of a subject. Thinking, such as lies at the basis of the lecture ("The Thing"), is no mere representing of some existent. "Being" is in no way identical with reality or with a precisely determined actuality. Nor is Being in any way opposed to being-no-longer and being-not-yet; these two belong themselves to the essential nature of Being. Even metaphysics already had, to a certain extent, an intimation of this fact in its doctrine of the modalities—which, to be sure, has hardly been understood—according to which possibility belongs to Being just as much as do actuality and necessity.

In thinking of Being, it is never the case that only something actual is represented in our minds and then given out as that which alone is true. To think "Being" means: to respond to the appeal of its presencing. The response stems from the appeal and releases itself toward that appeal. The responding is a giving way before the appeal and in this way an entering into its speech. But to the appeal of Being there also belongs the early uncovered has-been (*aletheia, logos, phusis*) as well as the veiled advent of what announces itself in the possible turnabout of the oblivion of Being (in the keeping of its nature). The responding must take into account all of this, on the strength of long concentration and in constant testing of its hearing, if it is to hear an appeal of Being. But precisely here the response may hear wrongly. In this thinking, the chance of going astray is greatest. This thinking can never show credentials such as mathematical knowledge can. But it is just as little a matter of arbitrariness; rather, it is rooted in the essential destiny of Being, though itself never compelling as a proposition. On the contrary, it is only a possible occasion to follow the path of responding, and indeed to follow it in the complete concentration of care and caution toward Being that language has *already* come to.

The default of God and the divinities is absence. But absence is not nothing; rather it is precisely the presence, which must first be appropriated, of the hidden fullness and wealth of what has been and what, thus gathered, is presencing, of the divine in the world of the Greeks, in prophetic Judaism, in the preaching of Jesus. This no-longer is in itself a not-yet of the veiled arrival of its inexhaustible nature. Since Being is never the merely precisely actual, to guard Being can never be equated with the task of a guard who protects from burglars a treasure stored in a building. Guardianship of Being is not fixated upon something existent. The existing thing, taken for itself, never contains an appeal of Being. Guardianship is vigilance, watchfulness for the has-been and coming destiny of Being, a vigilance that issues from a long and ever-renewed thoughtful deliberateness, which heeds the directive that lies in the manner in which Being makes its appeal. In the destiny of Being there is never a mere sequence of things one after another: now frame, then world and thing; rather, there is always a passing by and simultaneity of the early and late. In Hegel's *Phenome-nology of Spirit, aletheia* presences, though transmuted.

As a response, thinking of Being is a highly errant and in addition a very destitute matter. Thinking is perhaps, after all, an unavoidable path, which refuses to be a path of salvation and brings no new wisdom. The path is at most a field path, a path across fields, which does not just speak of renunciation but already has renounced, namely, renounced the claim to a binding doctrine and a valid cultural achievement or a deed of the spirit. Everything depends on the step back, fraught with error, into the thoughtful reflection that attends the turnabout of the oblivion of Being, the turnabout that is prefigured in the destiny of Being. The step back from the representational thinking of metaphysics does not reject such thinking, but opens the distant to the appeal of the trueness of Being in which the responding always takes place.

It has happened to me more than once, and indeed precisely with people close to me, that they listen gladly and attentively to the presentation of the jug's nature, but immediately stop listening when the discussion turns to objectness, the standing forth and coming forth of production—when it turns to framing. But all this is necessarily part of thinking of the thing, a thinking that thinks about the possible advent of world, and keeping it thus in mind perhaps helps, in the humblest and inconspicuous matters, such an advent to reach the opened-up realm of man's nature as man.

Among the curious experiences I have had with my lecture is also this, that someone raises the question as to whence my thinking gets its directive, as though this question were indicated in regard to this thinking alone. But it never occurs to anyone to ask whence Plato had a directive to think of Being as *idea,* or whence Kant had the directive to think of Being as the transcendental character of objectness, as position (being posited).

But maybe someday the answer to these questions can be

gained from those ventures of thought which, like mine, look as though they were lawless caprice.

I can provide no credentials for what I have said—which, indeed, you do not ask of me—that would permit a convenient check in each case whether what I say agrees with "reality."

Everything here is the path of a responding that examines as it listens. Any path always risks going astray, leading astray. To follow such paths takes practice in going. Practice needs craft. Stay on the path, in genuine need, and learn the craft of thinking, unswerving, yet erring.

Yours in friendship,

LANGUAGE

LANGUAGE

Man speaks. We speak when we are awake and we speak in our dreams. We are always speaking, even when we do not utter a single word aloud, but merely listen or read, and even when we are not particularly listening or speaking but are attending to some work or taking a rest. We are continually speaking in one way or another. We speak because speaking is natural to us. It does not first arise out of some special volition. Man is said to have language by nature. It is held that man, in distinction from plant and animal, is the living being capable of speech. This statement does not mean only that, along with other faculties, man also possesses the faculty of speech. It means to say that only speech enables man to be the living being he is as man. It is as one who speaks that man is—man. These are Wilhelm von Humboldt's words. Yet it remains to consider what it is to be called—man.

In any case, language belongs to the closest neighborhood of man's being. We encounter language everywhere. Hence it cannot surprise us that as soon as man looks thoughtfully about himself at what is, he quickly hits upon language too, so as to define it by a standard reference to its overt aspects. Reflection tries to obtain an idea of what language is universally. The universal that holds for each thing is called its essence or nature. To represent universally what holds universally is, according to prevalent views, the basic feature of thought. To deal with language thoughtfully would thus mean to give an idea of the nature of language and to distinguish this idea properly from other ideas. This lecture, too, seems to attempt something of that kind. However, the title of the lecture is not "On the Nature of Language." It is only "Language." "Only," we say, and yet we are clearly placing a far more presumptuous title at the head of our project than if we were to rest content with just making a few remarks about language. Still, to talk about language is presumably even worse than to write about silence. We do not wish to assault language in order to force it into the grip of ideas already fixed beforehand. We do not wish to reduce the nature of language to a concept, so that this concept may provide a generally useful view of language that will lay to rest all further notions about it.

To discuss language, to place it, means to bring to its place of being not so much language as ourselves: our own gathering into the appropriation.

We would reflect on language itself, and on language only. Language itself is—language and nothing else besides. Language itself is language. The understanding that is schooled in logic, thinking of everything in terms of calculation and hence usually overbearing, calls this proposition an empty tautology. Merely to say the identical thing twice—language is language—how is that supposed to get us anywhere? But we do not want to get anywhere. We would like only, for once, to get to just where we are already.

This is why we ponder the question, "What about language itself?" This is why we ask, "In what way does language occur as language?" We answer: *Language speaks.* Is this, seriously, an answer? Presumably—that is, when it becomes clear what speaking is.

To reflect on language thus demands that we enter into the speaking of language in order to take up our stay with language, i.e., within *its* speaking, not within our own. Only in that way do we arrive at the region within which it may happen—or also fail to happen—that language will call to us from there and grant us its nature. We leave the speaking to language. We do not wish to ground language in something else that is not language itself, nor do we wish to explain other things by means of language.

On the tenth of August, 1784 Hamann wrote to Herder (*Hamanns Schriften,* ed. Roth, VII, pp. 151 f.) * :

> If I were as eloquent as Demosthenes I would yet have to do nothing more than repeat a single word three times: reason is language, *logos.* I gnaw at this marrow-bone and will gnaw myself to death over it. There still remains a darkness, always, over this depth for me; I am still waiting for an apocalyptic angel with a key to this abyss.

For Hamann, this abyss consists in the fact that reason is language. Hamann returns to language in his attempt to say what reason is. His glance, aimed at reason, falls into the depths of an abyss. Does this abyss consist only in the fact that reason resides in language, or is language itself the abyss? We speak of an abyss where the ground falls away and a ground is lacking to us, where we seek the ground and set out to arrive at a ground, to get to the bottom of something. But we do not ask now what reason may be; here we reflect immediately on language and take as our main clue the curious statement, "Language is language." This statement does not lead us to something else in which language is grounded. Nor does it say anything about whether language itself may be a ground for something else. The sentence, "Language is language," leaves us to hover over an abyss as long as we endure what it says.

Language is—language, speech. Language speaks. If we let ourselves fall into the abyss denoted by this sentence, we do not go tumbling into emptiness. We fall upward, to a height. Its

* [Johann Georg Hamann. *Schriften.* Edited by F. Roth and G. A. Wiener. Berlin: G. Reimer, 1821. 8 Parts, the last in 2 subdivisions, VIIIa and VIIIb.—Tr.]

loftiness opens up a depth. The two span a realm in which we would like to become at home, so as to find a residence, a dwelling place for the life of man.

To reflect on language means—to reach the speaking of language in such a way that this speaking takes place as that which grants an abode for the being of mortals.

What does it mean to speak? The current view declares that speech is the activation of the organs for sounding and hearing. Speech is the audible expression and communication of human feelings. These feelings are accompanied by thoughts. In such a characterization of language three points are taken for granted:

First and foremost, speaking is expression. The idea of speech as an utterance is the most common. It already presupposes the idea of something internal that utters or externalizes itself. If we take language to be utterance, we give an external, surface notion of it at the very moment when we explain it by recourse to something internal.

Secondly, speech is regarded as an activity of man. Accordingly we have to say that man speaks, and that he always speaks some language. Hence we cannot say, "Language speaks." For this would be to say: "It is language that first brings man about, brings him into existence." Understood in this way, man would be bespoken by language.

Finally, human expression is always a presentation and representation of the real and the unreal.

It has long been known that the characteristics we have advanced do not suffice to circumscribe the nature of language. But when we understand the nature of language in terms of expression, we give it a more comprehensive definition by incorporating expression, as one among many activities, into the total economy of those achievements by which man makes himself.

As against the identification of speech as a merely human performance, others stress that the word of language is of divine origin. According to the opening of the Prologue of the Gospel of St. John, in the beginning the Word was with God. The attempt is made not only to free the question of origin from the fetters of a rational-logical explanation, but also to set aside the limits of a merely logical description of language. In opposition to the exclusive characterization of word-meanings as concepts, the figurative and symbolical character of language is pushed into the foreground. Biology and philosophical anthropology, sociology and psychopathology, theology and poetics are all then called upon to describe and explain linguistic phenomena more comprehensively.

In the meantime, all statements are referred in advance to the traditionaly standard way in which language appears. The already fixed view of the whole nature of language is thus consolidated. This is how the idea of language in grammar and logic, philosophy of language and linguistics, has remained the same for two and a half millennia, although knowledge about language has progressively increased and changed. This fact could even be adduced as evidence for the unshakable correctness of the leading ideas about language. No one would dare to declare incorrect, let alone reject as useless, the identification of language as audible utterance of inner emotions, as human activity, as a representation by image and by concept. The view of language thus put forth is correct, for it conforms to what an investigation of linguistic phenomena can make out in them at any time. And all *questions* associated with the description and explanation of linguistic phenomena also move within the precincts of this correctness.

We still give too little consideration, however, to the singular role of these correct ideas about language. They hold sway, as if unshakable, over the whole field of the varied scientific perspectives on language. They have their roots in an ancient tradition. Yet they ignore completely the oldest natural cast of language. Thus, despite their antiquity and despite their comprehensibility, they never bring us to language as language.

Language speaks. What about its speaking? Where do we

encounter such speaking? Most likely, to be sure, in what is spoken. For here speech has come to completion in what is spoken. The speaking does not cease in what is spoken. Speaking is kept safe in what is spoken. In what is spoken, speaking gathers the ways in which it persists as well as that which persists by it—its persistence, its presencing. But most often, and too often, we encounter what is spoken only as the residue of a speaking long past.

If we must, therefore, seek the speaking of language in what is spoken, we shall do well to find something that is spoken purely rather than to pick just any spoken material at random. What is spoken purely is that in which the completion of the speaking that is proper to what is spoken is, in its turn, an original. What is spoken purely is the poem. For the moment, we must let this statement stand as a bare assertion. We may do so, if we succeed in hearing in a poem something that is spoken purely. But what poem shall speak to us? Here we have only one choice, but one that is secured against mere caprice. By what? By what is already told us as the presencing element in language, if we follow in thought the speaking *of language*. Because of this bond between what we think and what we are told by language we choose, as something spoken purely, a poem which more readily than others can help us in our first steps to discover what is binding in that bond. We listen to what is spoken. The poem bears the title:

A Winter Evening

Window with falling snow is arrayed,
Long tolls the vesper bell,
The house is provided well,
The table is for many laid.

Wandering ones, more than a few,
Come to the door on darksome courses.

Golden blooms the tree of graces
Drawing up the earth's cool dew.

Wanderer quietly steps within;
Pain has turned the threshold to stone.
There lie, in limpid brightness shown,
Upon the table bread and wine.

The two last verses of the second stanza and the third stanza
read in the first version (Letter to Karl Kraus, December 13,
1913):

Love's tender power, full of graces,
Binds up his wounds anew.

O! man's naked hurt condign.
Wrestler with angels mutely held,
Craves, by holy pain compelled,
Silently God's bread and wine.

(Cf. the new Swiss edition of the poems of G. Trakl edited
by Kurt Horwitz, 1946.) *

The poem was written by Georg Trakl. Who the author is
remains unimportant here, as with every other masterful poem.
The mastery consists precisely in this, that the poem can deny
the poet's person and name.

The poem is made up of three stanzas. Their meter and rhyme
pattern can be defined accurately according to the schemes of
metrics and poetics. The poem's content is comprehensible.
There is not a single word which, taken by itself, would be un-

---

* [Georg Trakl, *Die Dichtungen. Gesamtausgabe mit einem Anhang:
Zeugnisse und Erinnerungen,* edited by Kurt Horwitz. Zürich: Arche Verlag,
1946. This poem, "Ein Winterabend," may also be found in *Die Dichtungen,*
11th edition. Salzburg: Otto Müller, 1938, p. 124. The letter to Karl Kraus
may be found in *Erinnerung an Georg Trakl: Zeugnisse und Briefe,* Salzburg: Otto Müller, 1959, pp. 172–173.—Tr.]

familiar or unclear. To be sure, a few of the verses sound strange, like the third and fourth in the second stanza:

> Golden blooms the tree of graces
> Drawing up the earth's cool dew.

Similarly, the second verse of the third stanza is startling:

> Pain has turned the threshold to stone.

But the verses here singled out also manifest a particular beauty of imagery. This beauty heightens the charm of the poem and strengthens its aesthetic perfection as an artistic structure.

The poem describes a winter evening. The first stanza describes what is happening outside: snowfall, and the ringing of the vesper bell. The things outside touch the things inside the human homestead. The snow falls on the window. The ringing of the bell enters into every house. Within, everything is well provided and the table set.

The second stanza raises a contrast. While many are at home within the house and at the table, not a few wander homeless on darksome paths. And yet such—possibly evil—roads sometimes lead to the door of the sheltering house. To be sure, this fact is not presented expressly. Instead, the poem names the tree of graces.

The third stanza bids the wanderer enter from the dark outdoors into the brightness within. The houses of the many and the tables of their daily meals have become house of God and altar.

The content of the poem might be dissected even more distinctly, its form outlined even more precisely, but in such operations we would still remain confined by the notion of language that has prevailed for thousands of years. According to this idea language is the expression, produced by men, of their feelings and the world view that guides them. Can the spell this idea has cast over language be broken? Why should it be

broken? In its essence, language is neither expression nor an activity of man. Language speaks. We are now seeking the speaking of language in the poem. Accordingly, what we seek lies in the poetry of the spoken word.

The poem's title is "A Winter Evening." We expect from it the description of a winter evening as it actually is. But the poem does not picture a winter evening occurring somewhere, sometime. It neither merely describes a winter evening that is already there, nor does it attempt to produce the semblance, leave the impression, of a winter evening's presence where there is no such winter evening. Naturally not, it will be replied. Everyone knows that a poem is an invention. It is imaginative even where it seems to be descriptive. In his fictive act the poet pictures to himself something that could be present in its presence. The poem, as composed, images what is thus fashioned for our own act of imaging. In the poem's speaking the poetic imagination gives itself utterance. What is spoken in the poem is what the poet enunciates out of himself. What is thus spoken out, speaks by enunciating its content. The language of the poem is a manifold enunciating. Language proves incontestably to be expression. But this conclusion is in conflict with the proposition "Language speaks," assuming that speaking, in its essential nature, is not an expressing.

Even when we understand what is spoken in the poem in terms of poetic composition, it seems to us, as if under some compulsion, always and only to be an expressed utterance. Language is expression. Why do we not reconcile ourselves to this fact? Because the correctness and currency of this view of language are insufficient to serve as a basis for an account of the nature of language. How shall we gauge this inadequacy? Must we not be bound by a different standard before we can gauge anything in that manner? Of course. That standard reveals itself in the proposition, "Language speaks." Up to this point this guiding proposition. has had merely the function of warding off the ingrained habit of disposing of speech by throwing it at once among the phenomena of expression instead of thinking it in its own terms. The poem cited has been chosen because, in a way not further explicable, it demonstrates a peculiar fitness to provide some fruitful hints for our attempt to discuss language.

Language *speaks*. This means at the same time and before all else: *language* speaks. Language? And not man? What our guiding proposition demands of us now—is it not even worse than before? Are we, in addition to everything else, also going to deny now that man is the being who speaks? Not at all. We deny this no more than we deny the possibility of classifying linguistic phenomena under the heading of "expression." But we ask, "How does man speak?" We ask, "What is it to speak?"

> Window with falling snow is arrayed
> Long tolls the vesper bell.

This speaking names the snow that soundlessly strikes the window late in the waning day, while the vesper bell rings. In such a snowfall, everything lasting lasts longer. Therefore the vesper bell, which daily rings for a strictly fixed time, tolls long. The speaking names the winter evening time. What is this naming? Does it merely deck out the imaginable familiar objects and events—snow, bell, window, falling, ringing—with words of a language? No. This naming does not hand out titles, it does not apply terms, but it calls into the word. The naming calls. Calling brings closer what it calls. However this bringing closer does not fetch what is called only in order to set it down in closest proximity to what is present, to find a place for it there. The call does indeed call. Thus it brings the presence of what was previously uncalled into a nearness. But the call, in calling it here, has already called out to what it calls. Where to? Into the distance in which what is called remains, still absent.

The calling here calls into a nearness. But even so the call does not wrest what it calls away from the remoteness, in which it is kept by the calling there. The calling calls into itself and therefore always here and there—here into presence, there into absence. Snowfall and tolling of vesper bell are spoken to us here and now in the poem. They are present in the call. Yet they in no way fall among the things present here and now in this lecture hall. Which presence is higher, that of these present things or the presence of what is called?

> The house is provided well,
> The table is for many laid.

The two verses speak like plain statements, as though they were noting something present. The emphatic "is" sounds that way. Nevertheless it speaks in the mode of calling. The verses bring the well-provided house and the ready table into that presence that is turned toward something absent.

What does the first stanza call? It calls things, bids them come. Where? Not to be present among things present; it does not bid the table named in the poem to be present here among the rows of seats where you are sitting. The place of arrival which is also called in the calling is a presence sheltered in absence. The naming call bids things to come into such an arrival. Bidding is inviting. It invites things in, so that they may bear upon men as things. The snowfall brings men under the sky that is darkening into night. The tolling of the evening bell brings them, as mortals, before the divine. House and table join mortals to the earth. The things that were named, thus called, gather to themselves sky and earth, mortals and divinities. The four are united primally in being toward one another, a fourfold. The things let the fourfold of the four stay with them. This gathering, assembling, letting-stay is the thinging of things. The unitary fourfold of sky and earth, mortals and divinities, which is stayed in the thinging of things, we call— the world. In the naming, the things named are called into their thinging. Thinging, they unfold world, in which things abide and so are the abiding ones. By thinging, things carry out world. Our old language calls such carrying *bern, bären*—Old High German *beran*—to bear; hence the words *gebaren,* to carry, gestate, give birth, and *Gebärde,* bearing, gesture. Thinging, things are things. Thinging, they gesture—gestate—world.

The first stanza calls things into their thinging, bids them come. The bidding that calls things calls them here, invites them, and at the same time calls out to the things, commending them to the world out of which they appear. Hence the first stanza names not only things. It simultaneously names world. It calls the "many" who belong as mortals to the world's fourfold. Things be-thing—i.e., condition—mortals. This now means: things, each in its time, literally visit mortals with a world. The first stanza speaks by bidding the things to come.

The second stanza speaks in a different way. To be sure, it too bids to come. But its calling begins as it calls and names mortals:

> Wandering ones, more than a few . . .

Not all mortals are called, not the many of the first stanza, but only "more than a few"—those who wander on dark courses. These mortals are capable of dying as the wandering toward death. In death the supreme concealedness of Being crystallizes. Death has already overtaken every dying. Those "wayfarers" must first wander their way to house and table through the darkness of their courses; they must do so not only and not even primarily for themselves, but for the many, because the many think that if they only install themselves in houses and sit at tables, they are already bethinged, conditioned, by things and have arrived at dwelling.

The second stanza begins by calling more than a few of the mortals. Although mortals belong to the world's fourfold along with the divinities, with earth and sky, the first two verses of the second stanza do not expressly call the world. Rather, very much like the first stanza but in a different sequence, they at the same time name things—the door, the dark paths. It is the two remaining verses that expressly name the world. Suddenly they name something wholly different:

> Golden blooms the tree of graces
> Drawing up the earth's cool dew.

The tree roots soundly in the earth. Thus it is sound and flourishes into a blooming that opens itself to heaven's blessing. The tree's towering has been called. It spans both the ecstasy of flowering and the soberness of the nourishing sap. The earth's abated growth and the sky's open bounty belong together. The poem names the tree of graces. Its sound blossoming harbors the fruit that falls to us unearned—holy, saving, loving toward mortals. In the golden-blossoming tree there prevail earth and sky, divinities and mortals. Their unitary fourfold is the world. The word "world" is now no longer used in the metaphysical sense. It designates neither the universe of nature and history in its secular representation nor the theologically conceived creation (*mundus*), nor does it mean simply the whole of entities present (*kosmos*).

The third and fourth lines of the second stanza call the tree of graces. They expressly bid the world to come. They call the world-fourfold here, and thus call world to the things.

The two lines start with the word "golden." So that we may hear more clearly this word and what it calls, let us recollect a poem of Pindar's: *Isthmians* V. At the beginning of this ode the poet calls gold *periosion panton,* that which above all shines through everything, *panta,* shines through each thing present all around. The splendor of gold keeps and holds everything present in the unconcealedness of its appearing.

As the calling that names things calls here and there, so the saying that names the world calls into itself, calling here and there. It entrusts world to the things and simultaneously keeps the things in the splendor of world. The world grants to things their presence. Things bear world. World grants things.

The speaking of the first two stanzas speaks by bidding things to come to world, and world to things. The two modes of bidding are different but not separated. But neither are they merely coupled together. For world and things do not subsist alongside one another. They penetrate each other. Thus the two traverse a middle. In it, they are at one. Thus at one they are intimate. The middle of the two is intimacy—in Latin, *inter*. The corresponding German word is *unter*, the English *inter*-. The intimacy of world and thing is not a fusion. Intimacy obtains only where the intimate—world and thing—divides itself cleanly and remains separated. In the midst of the two, in the between of world and thing, in their *inter*, division prevails: a *dif-ference*.

The intimacy of world and thing is present in the separation of the between; it is present in the dif-ference. The word difference is now removed from its usual and customary usage. What it now names is not a generic concept for various kinds of differences. It exists only as this single difference. It is unique. Of itself, it holds apart the middle in and through which world and things are at one with each other. The intimacy of the dif-ference is the unifying element of the *diaphora*, the carrying out that carries through. The dif-ference carries out world in its worlding, carries out things in their thinging. Thus carrying them out, it carries them toward one another. The dif-ference does not mediate after the fact by connecting world and things through a middle added on to them. Being the middle, it first determines world and things in their presence, i.e., in their being toward one another, whose unity it carries out.

The word consequently no longer means a distinction established between objects only by our representations. Nor is it merely a relation obtaining between world and thing, so that a representation coming upon it can establish it. The dif-ference is not abstracted from world and thing as their relationship after the fact. The dif-ference for world and thing *disclosingly appropriates* things into bearing a world; it *disclosingly appropriates* world into the granting of things.

The dif-ference is neither distinction nor relation. The dif-ference is, at most, dimension for world and thing. But in this case "dimension" also no longer means a precinct already present independently in which this or that comes to settle. The dif-ference is *the* dimension, insofar as it measures out, apportions, world and thing, each to its own. Its allotment of them first opens up the separateness and towardness of world and thing. Such an opening up is the way in which the dif-ference here spans the two. The dif-ference, as the middle for world and things, metes out the measure of their presence. In the bidding that calls thing and world, what is really called is: the dif-ference.

The first stanza of the poem bids the things to come which, thinging, bear world. The second stanza bids that world to come which, worlding, grants things. The third stanza bids the middle for world and things to come: the carrying out of the intimacy. On this account the third stanza begins with an emphatic calling:

Wanderer quietly steps within.

Where to? The verse does not say. Instead, it calls the entering wanderer into the stillness. This stillness ministers over the doorway. Suddenly and strangely the call sounds:

Pain has turned the threshold to stone.

This verse speaks all by itself in what is spoken in the whole poem. It names pain. What pain? The verse says merely "pain." Whence and in what way is pain called?

Pain has turned the threshold to stone.

"Turned . . . to stone"—these are the only words in the poem that speak in the past tense. Even so, they do not name something gone by, something no longer present. They name something that persists and that has already persisted. It is only in turning to stone that the threshold presences at all.

The threshold is the ground-beam that bears the doorway as a whole. It sustains the middle in which the two, the outside and the inside, penetrate each other. The threshold bears the between. What goes out and goes in, in the between, is joined in the between's dependability. The dependability of the middle must never yield either way. The settling of the between needs something that can endure, and is in this sense hard. The threshold, as the settlement of the between, is hard because pain has petrified it. But the pain that became appropriated to stone did not harden into the threshold in order to congeal there. The pain presences unflagging in the threshold, as pain.

But what is pain? Pain rends. It is the rift. But it does not tear apart into dispersive fragments. Pain indeed tears asunder, it separates, yet so that at the same time it draws everything to itself, gathers it to itself. Its rending, as a separating that gathers, is at the same time that drawing which, like the pen-drawing of a plan or sketch, draws and joins together what is held apart in separation. Pain is the joining agent in the rending that divides and gathers. Pain is the joining of the rift. The joining is the threshold. It settles the between, the middle of the two that are separated in it. Pain joins the rift of the dif-ference. Pain is the dif-ference itself.

Pain has turned the threshold to stone.

The verse calls the dif-ference, but it neither thinks it specifically nor does it call its nature by this name. The verse calls the separation of the between, the gathering middle, in whose intimacy the bearing of things and the granting of world pervade one another.

Then would the intimacy of the dif-ference for world and thing be pain? Certainly. But we should not imagine pain anthropologically as a sensation that makes us feel afflicted. We should not think of the intimacy psychologically as the sort in which sentimentality makes a nest for itself.

Pain has turned the threshold to stone.

Pain has already fitted the threshold into its bearing. The dif-ference presences already as the collected presence, from which the carrying out of world and thing appropriatingly takes place. How so?

There lie, in limpid brightness shown,
Upon the table bread and wine.

Where does the pure brightness shine? On the threshold, in the settling of the pain. The rift of the dif-ference makes the limpid brightness shine. Its luminous joining decides the brightening of the world into its own. The rift of the dif-ference expropriates the world into its worlding, which grants things. By the brightening of the world in their golden gleam, bread and wine at the same time attain to their own gleaming. The nobly named things are lustrous in the simplicity of their thinging. Bread and wine are the fruits of heaven and earth, gifts from the divinities to mortals. Bread and wine gather these four to themselves from the simple unity of their fourfoldness. The things that are called bread and wine are simple things because their bearing of world is fulfilled, without intermediary, by the favor of the world. Such things have their sufficiency in letting the world's fourfold stay with them. The pure limpid brightness of world and the simple gleaming of things go through their between, the dif-ference.

The third stanza calls world and things into the middle of their intimacy. The seam that binds their being toward one another is pain.

Only the third stanza gathers the bidding of things and the bidding of world. For the third stanza calls primally out of the simplicity of the intimate bidding which calls the dif-ference by leaving it unspoken. The primal calling, which bids the intimacy of world and thing to come, is the authentic bidding. This bidding is the nature of speaking. Speaking occurs in what is spoken in the poem. It is the speaking of language. Language speaks. It speaks by bidding the bidden, thing-world and world-thing, to come to the between of the dif-ference. What is so bidden is commanded to arrive from out of the dif-ference into the dif-ference. Here we are thinking of the old sense of command, which we recognize still in the phrase, "Commit thy way unto the Lord." The bidding of language commits the bidden thus to the bidding of the dif-ference. The dif-ference lets the thinging of the thing rest in the worlding of the world. The dif-ference expropriates the thing into the repose of the fourfold. Such expropriation does not diminish the thing. Only so is the thing exalted into its own, so that it stays world. To keep in repose is to still. The dif-ference stills the thing, as thing, into the world.

Such stilling, however, takes place only in such a way that at the same time the world's fourfold fulfills the bearing of the thing, in that the stilling grants to the thing the sufficiency of staying world. The dif-ference stills in a twofold manner. It stills by letting things rest in the world's favor. It stills by letting the world suffice itself in the thing. In the double stilling of the dif-ference there takes place: stillness.

What is stillness? It is in no way merely the soundless. In soundlessness there persists merely a lack of the motion of entoning, sounding. But the motionless is neither limited to sounding by being its suspension, nor is it itself already something genuinely tranquil. The motionless always remains, as it were, merely the other side of that which rests. The motionless itself still rests on rest. But rest has its being in the fact that it stills. As the stilling of stillness, rest, conceived strictly, is always more in motion than all motion and always more restlessly active than any agitation.

The dif-ference stills particularly in two ways: it stills the things in thinging and the world in worlding. Thus stilled, thing and world never escape from the dif-ference. Rather, they rescue it in the stilling, where the dif-ference is itself the stillness.

In stilling things and world into their own, the dif-ference calls world and thing into the middle of their intimacy. The dif-ference is the bidder. The dif-ference gathers the two out of itself as it calls them into the rift that is the dif-ference itself. This gathering calling is the pealing. In it there occurs something different from a mere excitation and spreading of sound.

When the dif-ference gathers world and things into the simple onefold of the pain of intimacy, it bids the two to come into their very nature. The dif-ference is the command out of which every bidding itself is first called, so that each may follow the command. The command of the dif-ference has ever already gathered all bidding within itself. The calling, gathered together with itself, which gathers to itself in the calling, is the pealing as the peal.

The calling of the dif-ference is the double stilling. The gathered bidding, the command, in the form of which the dif-ference calls world and things, is the peal of stillness. Language speaks in that the command of the dif-ference calls world and things into the simple onefold of their intimacy.

Language speaks as the peal of stillness. Stillness stills by the carrying out, the bearing and enduring, of world and things in their presence. The carrying out of world and thing in the manner of stilling is the appropriative taking place of the dif-ference. Language, the peal of stillness, is, inasmuch as the dif-ference takes place. Language goes on as the taking place or occurring of the dif-ference for world and things.

The peal of stillness is not anything human. But on the contrary, the human is indeed in its nature given to speech—it is linguistic. The word "linguistic" as it is here used means:

having taken place out of the speaking of language. What has thus taken place, human being, has been brought into its own by language, so that it remains given over or appropriated to the nature of language, the peal of stillness. Such an appropriating takes place in that the very *nature,* the *presencing,* of language *needs and uses* the speaking of mortals in order to sound as the peal of stillness for the hearing of mortals. Only as men belong within the peal of stillness are mortals able to speak in *their own* way in sounds.

Mortal speech is a calling that names, a bidding which, out of the simple onefold of the difference, bids thing and world to come. What is purely bidden in mortal speech is what is spoken in the poem. Poetry proper is never merely a higher mode (*melos*) of everyday language. It is rather the reverse: everyday language is a forgotten and therefore used-up poem, from which there hardly resounds a call any longer.

The opposite of what is purely spoken, the opposite of the poem, is not prose. Pure prose is never "prosaic." It is as poetic and hence as rare as poetry.

If attention is fastened exclusively on human speech, if human speech is taken simply to be the voicing of the inner man, if speech so conceived is regarded as language itself, then the nature of language can never appear as anything but an expression and an activity of man. But human speech, as the speech of mortals, is not self-subsistent. The speech of mortals rests in its relation to the speaking of language.

At the proper time it becomes unavoidable to think of how mortal speech and its utterance take place in the speaking of language as the peal of the stillness of the dif-ference. Any uttering, whether in speech or writing, breaks the stillness. On what does the peal of stillness break? How does the broken stillness come to sound in words? How does the broken stillness shape the mortal speech that sounds in verses and sentences?

Assuming that thinking will succeed one day in answering

these questions, it must be careful not to regard utterance, let alone expression, as the decisive element of human speech.

The structure of human speech can only be the manner (*melos*) in which the speaking of language, the peal of the stillness of the dif-ference, appropriates mortals by the command of the dif-ference.

The way in which mortals, called out of the dif-ference into the dif-ference, speak on their own part, is: by responding. Mortal speech must first of all have listened to the command, in the form of which the stillness of the dif-ference calls world and things into the rift of its onefold simplicity. Every word of mortal speech speaks out of such a listening, and as such a listening.

Mortals speak insofar as they listen. They heed the bidding call of the stillness of the dif-ference even when they do not know that call. Their listening draws from the command of the dif-ference what it brings out as sounding word. This speaking that listens and accepts is responding.

Nevertheless by receiving what it says from the command of the dif-ference, mortal speech has already, in its own way, followed the call. Response, as receptive listening, is at the same time a recognition that makes due acknowledgment. Mortals speak by responding to language in a twofold way, receiving and replying. The mortal word speaks by cor-responding in a multiple sense.

Every authentic hearing holds back with its own saying. For hearing keeps to itself in the listening by which it remains appropriated to the peal of stillness. All responding is attuned to this restraint that reserves itself. For this reason such reserve must be concerned to be ready, in the mode of listening, for the command of the dif-ference. But the reserve must take care not just to hear the peal of stillness afterward, but to hear it even beforehand, and thus as it were to anticipate its command.

This anticipating while holding back determines the manner

in which mortals respond to the dif-ference. In this way mortals live in the speaking of language.

Language speaks. Its speaking bids the dif-ference to come which expropriates world and things into the simple onefold of their intimacy.

Language speaks.

Man speaks in that he responds to language. This responding is a hearing. It hears because it listens to the command of still-ness.

It is not a matter here of stating a new view of language. What is important is learning to live in the speaking of language. To do so, we need to examine constantly whether and to what extent we are capable of what genuinely belongs to re-sponding: anticipation in reserve. For:

> Man speaks only as he responds to language.
> Language speaks.
> Its speaking speaks for us in what has been spoken:

A Winter Evening

> Window with falling snow is arrayed,
> Long tolls the vesper bell,
> The house is provided well,
> The table is for many laid.
>
> Wandering ones, more than a few,
> Come to the door on darksome courses.
> Golden blooms the tree of graces
> Drawing up the earth's cool dew.
>
> Wanderer quietly steps within;
> Pain has turned the threshold to stone.
> There lie, in limpid brightness shown,
> Upon the table bread and wine.

"... POETICALLY MAN DWELLS ..."

". . . POETICALLY MAN DWELLS . . ."

The phrase is taken from a late poem by Hölderlin, which comes to us by a curious route. It begins: "In lovely blueness blooms the steeple with metal roof." (Stuttgart edition 2, 1, pp. 372 ff.; Hellingrath VI, pp. 24 ff.) If we are to hear the phrase "poetically man dwells" rightly, we must restore it thoughtfully to the poem. For that reason let us give thought to the phrase. Let us clear up the doubts it immediately arouses. For otherwise we should lack the free readiness to respond to the phrase by following it.

". . . poetically man dwells . . ." If need be, we can imagine that poets do on occasion dwell poetically. But how is "man"—and this means every man and all the time—supposed to dwell poetically? Does not all dwelling remain incompatible with the poetic? Our dwelling is harassed by the housing shortage. Even if that were not so, our dwelling today is harassed by work, made insecure by the hunt for gain and success, bewitched by the entertainment and recreation industry. But when there is still room left in today's dwelling for the poetic, and time is still set aside, what comes to pass is at best a preoccupation with aestheticizing, whether in writing or on the air. Poetry is either rejected as a frivolous mooning and vaporizing into the unknown, and a flight into dreamland, or is counted as a part of literature. And the validity of literature is assessed by the latest prevailing standard. The prevailing standard, in turn, is made and controlled by the organs for making public civilized opinions. One of its functionaries—at once driver and driven —is the literature industry. In such a setting poetry cannot appear otherwise than as literature. Where it is studied entirely in educational and scientific terms, it is the object of literary history. Western poetry goes under the general heading of "European literature."

But if the sole form in which poetry exists is literary to start with, then how can human dwelling be understood as based on the poetic? The phrase, "man dwells poetically," comes indeed from a mere poet, and in fact from one who, we are told, could not cope with life. It is the way of poets to shut their eyes to actuality. Instead of acting, they dream. What they make is merely imagined. The things of imagination are merely made. Making is, in Greek, *poiesis*. And man's dwelling is supposed to be poetry and poetic? This can be assumed, surely, only by someone who stands aside from actuality and does not want to see the existent condition of man's historical-social life today— the sociologists call it the collective.

But before we so bluntly pronounce dwelling and poetry incompatible, it may be well to attend soberly to the poet's statement. It speaks of man's dwelling. It does not describe today's dwelling conditions. Above all, it does not assert that to dwell means to occupy a house, a dwelling place. Nor does it say that the poetic exhausts itself in an unreal play of poetic imagination. What thoughtful man, therefore, would presume to declare, unhesitatingly and from a somewhat dubious elevation, that dwelling and the poetic are incompatible? Perhaps the two can bear with each other. This is not all. Perhaps one even bears the other in such a way that dwelling rests on the poetic. If this is indeed what we suppose, then we are required to think of dwelling and poetry in terms of their essential nature. If we do not balk at this demand, we think of what is usually called the existence of man in terms of dwelling. In doing so, we do of course give up the customary notion of dwelling. According to that idea, dwelling remains merely one form of human behavior alongside many others. We work in the city, but dwell outside it. We travel, and dwell now here, now there. Dwelling so understood is always merely the occupying of a lodging.

When Hölderlin speaks of dwelling, he has before his eyes the basic character of human existence. He sees the "poetic," moreover, by way of its relation to this dwelling, thus understood essentially.

This does not mean, though, that the poetic is merely an ornament and bonus added to dwelling. Nor does the poetic character of dwelling mean merely that the poetic turns up in some way or other in all dwelling. Rather, the phrase "poetically man dwells" says: poetry first causes dwelling to be dwelling. Poetry is what really lets us dwell. But through what do we attain to a dwelling place? Through building. Poetic creation, which lets us dwell, is a kind of building.

Thus we confront a double demand: for one thing, we are to think of what is called man's existence by way of the nature of dwelling; for another, we are to think of the nature of poetry as a letting-dwell, as a—perhaps even *the*—distinctive kind of building. If we search out the nature of poetry according to this viewpoint, then we arrive at the nature of dwelling.

But where do we humans get our information about the nature of dwelling and poetry? Where does man generally get the claim to arrive at the nature of something? Man can make such a claim only where he receives it. He receives it from the telling of language. Of course, only when and only as long as he respects language's own nature. Meanwhile, there rages round the earth an unbridled yet clever talking, writing, and broadcasting of spoken words. Man acts as though he were the shaper and master of language, while in fact language remains the master of man. When this relation of dominance gets inverted, man hits upon strange maneuvers. Language becomes the means of expression. As expression, language can decay into a mere medium for the printed word. That even in such employment of language we retain a concern for care in speaking is all to the good. But this alone will never help us to escape from the inversion of the true relation of dominance between language and man. For, strictly, it is language that speaks. Man first speaks when, and only when, he responds to language by listening to its appeal. Among all the appeals that we human beings, on our part, may help to be voiced, language is the highest and everywhere the first. Language beckons us, at first and then again at the end, toward a thing's nature. But that is not to say, ever, that in any word-meaning picked up at will language supplies us, straight away and definitively, with the transparent nature of the matter as if it were an object ready for use. But the responding in which man authentically listens to the appeal of language is that which speaks in the element of poetry. The more poetic a poet is— the freer (that is, the more open and ready for the unforeseen) his saying—the greater is the purity with which he submits what he says to an ever more painstaking listening, and the further what he says is from the mere propositional statement that is dealt with solely in regard to its correctness or incorrectness.

" . . . poetically man dwells . . . "

says the poet. We hear Hölderlin's words more clearly when we take them back into the poem in which they belong. First, let us listen only to the two lines from which we have detached and thus clipped the phrase. They run:

> Full of merit, yet poetically, man
> Dwells on this earth.

The keynote of the lines vibrates in the word "poetically." This word is set off in two directions: by what comes before it and by what follows.

Before it are the words: "Full of merit, yet . . . ." They sound almost as if the next word, "poetically," introduced a restriction on the profitable, meritorious dwelling of man. But it is just the reverse. The restriction is denoted by the expression "Full of merit," to which we must add in thought a "to be sure." Man, to be sure, merits and earns much in his dwelling. For he cultivates the growing things of the earth and takes care of his increase. Cultivating and caring (*colere, cultura*) are a kind of building. But man not only cultivates what produces growth out of itself; he also builds in the sense of *aedificare,* by erecting things that cannot come into being and subsist by growing. Things that are built in this sense include not only buildings but all the works made by man's hands and through his arrangements. Merits due to this building, however, can never fill out the nature of dwelling. On the contrary, they even deny dwelling its own nature when they are pursued and acquired purely for their own sake. For in that case these merits, precisely by their abundance, would everywhere constrain dwelling within the bounds of this kind of building. Such building pursues the fulfillment of the needs of dwelling. Building in the sense of the farmer's cultivation of growing things, and of the erecting of edifices and works and the production of tools, is already a consequence of the nature of dwelling, but it is not its ground, let alone its grounding. This grounding must take place in a different building. Building of the usual kind, often practiced exclusively and therefore the only one that is familiar, does of course bring an abundance of merits into dwelling. Yet man is capable of dwelling only if he has already built, is building, and remains disposed to build, in another way.

"Full of merit (to be sure), yet poetically, man dwells. . . ." This is followed in the text by the words: "on this earth." We might be inclined to think the addition superfluous; for dwelling, after all, already means man's stay on earth— on "this" earth, to which every mortal knows himself to be entrusted and exposed.

But when Hölderlin ventures to say that the dwelling of mortals is poetic, this statement, as soon as it is made, gives the impression that, on the contrary, "poetic" dwelling snatches man away from the earth. For the "poetic," when it is taken as poetry, is supposed to belong to the realm of fantasy. Poetic dwelling flies fantastically above reality. The poet counters this misgiving by saying expressly that poetic dwelling is a dwelling "on this earth." Hölderlin thus not only protects the "poetic" from a likely misinterpretation, but by adding the words "on this earth" expressly points to the nature of poetry. Poetry does not fly above and surmount the earth in order to escape it and hover over it. Poetry is what first brings man onto the earth, making him belong to it, and thus brings him into dwelling.

> Full of merit, yet poetically, man
> Dwells on this earth.

Do we know now why man dwells poetically? We still do not. We now even run the risk of intruding foreign thoughts into Hölderlin's poetic words. For Hölderlin indeed speaks of man's dwelling and his merit, but still he does not connect dwelling with building, as we have just done. He does not speak of building, either in the sense of cultivating and erecting, or in such a way as even to represent poetry as a special kind of building. Accordingly, Hölderlin does not speak of poetic dwelling as our own thinking does. Despite all this, we are thinking the same thing that Hölderlin is saying poetically.

It is, however, important to take note here of an essential point. A short parenthetical remark is needed. Poetry and thinking meet each other in one and the same only when, and only as long as, they remain distinctly in the distinctness of their nature. The same never coincides with the equal, not even in the empty indifferent oneness of what is merely identical. The equal or identical always moves toward the absence of difference, so that everything may be reduced to a common denominator. The same, by contrast, is the belonging together of what differs, through a gathering by way of the difference. We can only say "the same" if we think difference. It is in the carrying out and settling of differences that the gathering nature of sameness comes to light. The same banishes all zeal always to level what is different into the equal or identical. The same gathers what is distinct into an orginal being-at-one. The equal, on the contrary, disperses them into the dull unity of mere uniformity. Hölderlin, in his own way, knew of these relations. In an epigram which bears the title "Root of All Evil" (Stuttgart edition, I, 1, p. 305) he says:

> Being at one is godlike and good; whence, then,
> this craze among men that there should exist only
> One, why should all be one?

When we follow in thought Hölderlin's poetic statement about the poetic dwelling of man, we divine a path by which, through what is thought differently, we come nearer to thinking the same as what the poet composes in his poem.

But what does Hölderlin say of the poetic dwelling of man? We seek the answer to the question by listening to lines 24 to 38 of our poem. For the two lines on which we first commented are spoken from their region. Hölderlin says:

> May, if life is sheer toil, a man
> Lift his eyes and say: so
> I too wish to be? Yes. As long as Kindness,
> The Pure, still stays with his heart, man
> Not unhappily measures himself
> Against the godhead. Is God unknown?
> Is he manifest like the sky? I'd sooner
> Believe the latter. It's the measure of man.
> Full of merit, yet poetically, man
> Dwells on this earth. But no purer
> Is the shade of the starry night,
> If I might put it so, than
> Man, who's called an image of the godhead.

Is there a measure on earth? There is
None.

We shall think over only a few points in these lines, and for
the sole purpose of hearing more clearly what Hölderlin means
when he calls man's dwelling a "poetic" one. The first lines
(24 to 26) give us a clue. They are in the form of a question
that is answered confidently in the affirmative. The question is
a paraphrase of what the lines already expounded utter directly:
"Full of merit, yet poetically, man dwells on this earth." Hölderlin asks:

> May, if life is sheer toil, a man
> Lift his eyes and say: so
> I too wish to be? Yes.

Only in the realm of sheer toil does man toil for "merits."
There he obtains them for himself in abundance. But at the
same time, in this realm, man is allowed to look up, out of it,
through it, toward the divinities. The upward glance passes aloft
toward the sky, and yet it remains below on the earth. The upward glance spans the between of sky and earth. This between
is measured out for the dwelling of man. We now call the span
thus meted out the dimension. This dimension does not arise
from the fact that sky and earth are turned toward one another.
Rather, their facing each other itself depends on the dimension.
Nor is the dimension a stretch of space as ordinarily understood;
for everything spatial, as something for which space is made, is
already in need of the dimension, that is, that into which it is
admitted.

The nature of the dimension is the meting out—which is
lightened and so can be spanned—of the between: the upward
to the sky as well as the downward to earth. We leave the nature
of the dimension without a name. According to Hölderlin's
words, man spans the dimension by measuring himself against

the heavenly. Man does not undertake this spanning just now and then; rather, man is man at all only in such spanning. This is why he can indeed block this spanning, trim it, and disfigure it, but he can never evade it. Man, as man, has always measured himself with and against something heavenly. Lucifer, too, is descended from heaven. Therefore we read in the next lines (28 to 29): "Man measures himself against the godhead." The godhead is the "measure" with which man measures out his dwelling, his stay on the earth beneath the sky. Only insofar as man takes the measure of his dwelling in this way is he able to *be* commensurately with his nature. Man's dwelling depends on an upward-looking measure-taking of the dimension, in which the sky belongs just as much as the earth.

This measure-taking not only takes the measure of the earth, *ge,* and accordingly it is no mere geo-metry. Just as little does it ever take the measure of heaven, *ouranos,* for itself. Measure-taking is no science. Measure-taking gauges the between, which brings the two, heaven and earth, to one another. This measure-taking has its own *metron,* and thus its own metric.

Man's taking measure in the dimension dealt out to him brings dwelling into its ground plan. Taking the measure of the dimension is the element within which human dwelling has its security, by which it securely endures. The taking of measure is what is poetic in dwelling. Poetry is a measuring. But what is it to measure? If poetry is to be understood as measuring, then obviously we may not subsume it under just any idea of measuring and measure.

Poetry is presumably a high and special kind of measuring. But there is more. Perhaps we have to pronounce the sentence, "Poetry is a *measuring,*" with a different stress. "*Poetry* is a measuring." In poetry there takes place what all measuring is in the ground of its being. Hence it is necessary to pay heed to the basic act of measuring. That consists in man's first of all taking the measure which then is applied in every measuring act. In poetry the taking of measure occurs. To write poetry is measure-taking, understood in the strict sense of the word, by which man first receives the measure for the breadth of his being. Man exists as a mortal. He is called mortal because he can die. To be able to die means: to be capable of death as death. Only man dies—and indeed continually, so long as he stays on this earth, so long as he dwells. His dwelling, however, rests in the poetic. Hölderlin sees the nature of the "poetic" in the taking of the measure by which the measure-taking of human being is accomplished.

Yet how shall we prove that Hölderlin thinks of the nature of poetry as taking measure? We do not need to prove anything here. All proof is always only a subsequent undertaking on the basis of presuppositions. Anything at all can be proved, depending only on what presuppositions are made. But we can here pay heed only to a few points. It is enough, then, if we attend to the poet's own words. For in the next lines Hölderlin inquires, before anything else and in fact exclusively, as to man's measure. That measure is the godhead against which man measures himself. The question begins in line 29 with the words: "Is God unknown?" Manifestly not. For if he were unknown, how could he, being unknown, ever be the measure? Yet—and this is what we must now listen to and keep in mind—for Hölderlin God, as the one who he is, is unknown and it is just as *this Unknown One* that he is the measure for the poet. This is also why Hölderlin is perplexed by the exciting question: how can that which by its very nature remains unknown ever become a measure? For something that man measures himself by must after all impart itself, must appear. But if it appears, it is known. The god, however, is unknown, and he is the measure nonetheless. Not only this, but the god who remains unknown, must by showing *himself* as the one he is, appear as the one who remains unknown. God's *manifestness*—not only he himself—is mysterious. Therefore the poet immediately asks the next question: "Is he manifest like the sky?" Hölderlin answers: "I'd sooner/Believe the latter."

Why—so *we* now ask—is the poet's surmise inclined in that

way? The very next words give the answer. They say tersely: "It's the measure of man." What is the measure for human measuring? God? No. The sky? No. The manifestness of the sky? No. The measure consists in the way in which the god who remains unknown, is revealed *as* such by the sky. God's appearance through the sky consists in a disclosing that lets us see what conceals itself, but lets us see it not by seeking to wrest what is concealed out of its concealedness, but only by guarding the concealed in its self-concealment. Thus the unknown god appears as the unknown by way of the sky's manifestness. This appearance is the measure against which man measures himself.

A strange measure, perplexing it would seem to the common notions of mortals, inconvenient to the cheap omniscience of everyday opinion, which likes to claim that it is the standard for all thinking and reflection.

A strange measure for ordinary and in particular also for all merely scientific ideas, certainly not a palpable stick or rod but in truth simpler to handle than they, provided our hands do not abruptly grasp but are guided by gestures befitting the measure here to be taken. This is done by a taking which at no time clutches at the standard but rather takes it in a concentrated perception, a gathered taking-in, that remains a listening.

But why should this measure, which is so strange to us men of today, be addressed to man and imparted by the measure-taking of poetry? Because only this measure gauges the very nature of man. For man dwells by spanning the "on the earth" and the "beneath the sky." This "on" and "beneath" belong together. Their interplay is the span that man traverses at every moment insofar as he *is* as an earthly being. In a fragment (Stuttgart edition, 2, 1, p. 334) Hölderlin says:

> Always, love! the earth
> moves and heaven holds.

Because man *is,* in his enduring the dimension, his being must now and again be measured out. That requires a measure which involves at once the whole dimension in one. To discern this measure, to gauge it as the measure, and to accept it as the measure, means for the poet to make poetry. Poetry is this measure-taking—its taking, indeed, for the dwelling of man. For immediately after the words "It's the measure of man" there follow the lines: "Full of merit, yet poetically, man dwells on this earth."

Do we now know what the "poetic" is for Hölderlin? Yes and no. Yes, because we receive an intimation about how poetry is to be thought of: namely, it is to be conceived as a distinctive kind of measuring. No, because poetry, as the gauging of that strange measure, becomes ever more mysterious. And so it must doubtless remain, if we are really prepared to make our stay in the domain of poetry's being.

Yet it strikes us as strange that Hölderlin thinks of poetry as a measuring. And rightly so, as long as we understand measuring only in the sense current *for us*. In this sense, by the use of something known—measuring rods and their number—something unknown is stepped off and thus made known, and so is confined within a quantity and order which can always be determined at a glance. Such measuring can vary with the type of apparatus employed. But who will guarantee that this customary kind of measuring, merely because it is common, touches the nature of measuring? When we hear of measure, we immediately think of number and imagine the two, measure and number, as quantitative. But the *nature* of measure is no more a quantum than is the *nature* of number. True, we can reckon with numbers—but not with the nature of number. When Hölderlin envisages poetry as a measuring, and above all himself achieves poetry as taking measure, then we, in order to think of poetry, must ever and again first give thought to the measure that is taken in poetry; we must pay heed to the kind of taking here, which does not consist in a clutching or any other kind of grasping, but rather in a letting come of what has been dealt out. What is the measure for poetry? The godhead; God, therefore? Who is the god? Perhaps this question is too hard for man, and asked too soon. Let us therefore first ask what may be said about God. Let us first ask merely: What is God?

Fortunately for us, and helpfully, some verses of Hölderlin's have been preserved which belong in substance and time to the ambience of the poem "In lovely blueness. . . ." They begin (Stuttgart edition, 2, 1, p. 210):

> What is God? Unknown, yet
> Full of his qualities is the
> Face of the sky. For the lightnings
> Are the wrath of a god. The more something
> Is invisible, the more it yields to what's alien.

What remains alien to the god, the sight of the sky—this is what is familiar to man. And what is that? Everything that shimmers and blooms in the sky and thus under the sky and thus on earth, everything that sounds and is fragrant, rises and comes—but also everything that goes and stumbles, moans and falls silent, pales and darkens. Into this, which is intimate to man but alien to the god, the unknown imparts himself, in order to remain guarded within it as the unknown. But the poet calls all the brightness of the sights of the sky and every sound of its courses and breezes into the singing word and there makes them shine and ring. Yet the poet, if he is a poet, does not describe the mere appearance of sky and earth. The poet calls, in the sights of the sky, that which in its very self-disclosure causes the appearance of that which conceals itself, and indeed *as* that which conceals itself. In the familiar appearances, the poet calls the alien as that to which the invisible imparts itself in order to remain what it is—unknown.

The poet makes poetry only when he takes the measure, by saying the sights of heaven in such a way that he submits to its appearances as to the alien element to which the unknown god has "yielded." Our current name for the sight and appearance of something is "image." The nature of the image is to let something be seen. By contrast, copies and imitations are already mere variations on the genuine image which, as a sight or spectacle, lets the invisible be seen and so imagines the invisible in something alien to it. Because poetry takes that mysterious measure, to wit, in the face of the sky, therefore it speaks in "images." This is why poetic images are imaginings in a distinctive sense: not mere fancies and illusions but imaginings that are visible inclusions of the alien in the sight of the familiar. The poetic saying of images gathers the brightness and sound of the heavenly appearances into one with the darkness and silence of what is alien. By such sights the god surprises us. In this strangeness he proclaims his unfaltering nearness. For that reason Hölderlin, after the lines "Full of merit, yet poetically, man Dwells on this earth," can continue:

>   . . . Yet no purer
> Is the shade of the starry night,
> If I might put it so, than
> Man, who's called an image of the godhead.

"The shade of the night"—the night itself is the shade, that darkness which can never become a mere blackness because as shade it is wedded to light and remains cast by it. The measure taken by poetry yields, imparts itself—as the foreign element in which the invisible one preserves his presence—to what is familiar in the sights of the sky. Hence, the measure is of the same nature as the sky. But the sky is not sheer light. The radiance of its height is itself the darkness of its all-sheltering breadth. The blue of the sky's lovely blueness is the color of depth. The radiance of the sky is the dawn and dusk of the twilight, which shelters everything that can be proclaimed. This sky is the measure. This is why the poet must ask:

> Is there a measure on earth?

And he must reply: "There is none." Why? Because what we signify when we say "on the earth" exists only insofar as man dwells on the earth and in his dwelling lets the earth be as earth.

But dwelling occurs only when poetry comes to pass and is present, and indeed in the way whose nature we now have some idea of, as taking a measure for all measuring. This measure-taking is itself an authentic measure-taking, no mere gauging with ready-made measuring rods for the making of maps. Nor is poetry building in the sense of raising and fitting buildings. But poetry, as the authentic gauging of the dimension of dwelling, is the primal form of building. Poetry first of all admits man's dwelling into its very nature, its presencing being. Poetry is the original admission of dwelling.

The statement, *Man dwells in that he builds,* has now been given its proper sense. Man does not dwell in that he merely establishes his stay on the earth beneath the sky, by raising growing things and simultaneously raising buildings. Man is capable of such building only if he already builds in the sense of the poetic taking of measure. Authentic building occurs so far as there are poets, such poets as take the measure for architecture, the structure of dwelling.

On March 12, 1804 Hölderlin writes from Nürtingen to his friend Leo von Seckendorf: "At present I am especially occupied with the fable, the poetic view of history, and the architectonics of the skies, especially of our nation's, so far as it differs from the Greek" (Hellingrath V², p. 333).

" . . . poetically, man dwells . . . . "

Poetry builds up the very nature of dwelling. Poetry and dwelling not only do not exclude each other; on the contrary, poetry and dwelling belong together, each calling for the other. "Poetically man dwells." Do *we* dwell poetically? Presumably we dwell altogether unpoetically. If that is so, does it give the lie to the poet's words; are they untrue? No. The truth of his utterance is confirmed in the most unearthly way. For dwelling can be unpoetic only because it is in essence poetic. For a man to be blind, he must remain a being by nature endowed with sight. A piece of wood can never go blind. But when man goes blind, there always remains the question whether his blindness derives from some defect and loss or lies in an abundance and excess. In the same poem that meditates on the measure for all measuring, Hölderlin says (lines 75–76): "King Oedipus has perhaps one eye too many." Thus it might be that our unpoetic dwelling, its incapacity to take the measure, derives from a curious excess of frantic measuring and calculating.

That we dwell unpoetically, and in what way, we can in any case learn only if we know the poetic. Whether, and when, we may come to a turning point in our unpoetic dwelling is something we may expect to happen only if we remain heedful of the poetic. How and to what extent our doings can share in this turn we alone can prove, if we take the poetic seriously.

The poetic is the basic capacity for human dwelling. But man is capable of poetry at any time only to the degree to which his being is appropriate to that which itself has a liking for man and therefore needs his presence. Poetry is authentic or inauthentic according to the degree of this appropriation.

That is why authentic poetry does not come to light appropriately in every period. When and for how long does authentic poetry exist? Hölderlin gives the answer in verses 26–69, already cited. Their explication has been purposely deferred until now. The verses run:

> . . . As long as Kindness,
> The Pure, still stays with his heart, man
> Not unhappily measures himself
> Against the Godhead. . . .

"Kindness"—what is it? A harmless word, but described by Hölderlin with the capitalized epithet "the Pure." "Kindness"—

this word, if we take it literally, is Hölderlin's magnificent translation for the Greek word *charis*. In his *Ajax*, Sophocles says of *charis* (verse 522):

Charis charin gar estin he tiktous aei.

For kindness it is, that ever calls forth kindness.

"As long as Kindness, the Pure, still stays with his heart . . . ." Hölderlin says in an idiom he liked to use: "with his heart," not "in his heart." That is, it has come to the dwelling being of man, come as the claim and appeal of the measure to the heart in such a way that the heart turns to give heed to the measure.

As long as this arrival of kindness endures, so long does man succeed in measuring himself not unhappily against the godhead. When this measuring appropriately comes to light, man creates poetry from the very nature of the poetic. When the poetic appropriately comes to light, then man dwells humanly on this earth, and then—as Hölderlin says in his last poem—"the life of man" is a "dwelling life" (Stuttgart edition, 2, 1, p. 312).

Vista

When far the dwelling life of man into the distance goes,
Where, in that far distance, the grapevine's season glows,
There too are summer's fields, emptied of their growing,
And forest looms, its image darkly showing.
That Nature paints the seasons so complete,
That she abides, but they glide by so fleet,
Comes of perfection; then heaven's radiant height
Crowns man, as blossoms crown the trees, with light.

72 73 10 9 8 7 6 5 4 3 2